THE FABLES OF PHAEDRUS

D0937598

The Fables
of Phaedrus

TRANSLATED BY
P. F. WIDDOWS

UNIVERSITY OF TEXAS PRESS
Austin

Copyright © 1992 by the University of Texas Press
All rights reserved
Printed in the United States of America

First Edition, 1992

Requests for permission to reproduce material from this
work should be sent to Permissions, University of Texas
Press, Box 7819, Austin, Texas 78713-7819.

⊗ The paper used in this publication meets the
minimum requirements of American National Standard
for Information Sciences—Permanence of Paper for
Printed Library Materials, ANSI Z39.48-1984.

Design and typography by George Lenox

LIBRARY OF CONGRESS
CATALOGING-IN-PUBLICATION DATA

Phaedrus.
  [Fabulae. English]
  The fables of Phaedrus / translated by P. F. Widdows.
  — 1st ed.
    p.   cm.
  Translation of: Fabulae.
  Includes bibliographical references.
  ISBN 0-292-72470-5 (cloth). — ISBN 0-292-72473-X (paper)
  1. Phaedrus—Translations into English. 2. Fables,
Latin—Translations into English. I. Widdows, P. F.
(Paul Frederick), 1918– . II. Title.
PA6564.E5W5 1992
871'.01—dc20   91-9765
                                  CIP

CONTENTS

BOOK 5

PEROTTI'S APPENDIX

INTRODUCTION

Life and Works

Almost all our information about Phaedrus, the Roman fabulist of the period of Augustus and Tiberius, is derived from his work itself, some of it directly, some of it by deduction. Outside that there is only one contribution, but it is an important one. It comes from the only surviving manuscript of Phaedrus, the Codex Pithoeanus (ninth century A.D.), which entitles the collection *Phaedri, Augusti liberti, fabularum aesopiarum libri* [*The Books of Aesopic Fables by Phaedrus, the Freedman of Augustus*]. That is to say, he was a slave in the household of Augustus and at some point was granted his freedom by the emperor. This is nowhere stated in the poems, although the fact of his having been a slave is supported by his expression of admiration for the figure of Aesop, the traditional originator of the genre of fable:

> The Athenians set up a statue to Aesop,
> Thereby placing a slave on a permanent pedestal
> To the end that all should openly acknowledge
> That glory is granted to greatness, not to birth.
>
> (2, 9, 1–4)

More can be elicited from the poems themselves. We can know or deduce:

— That he was born in Pieria (the traditional home of the Muses) in Thessaly, which was at that time part of a Roman province.

— That he was possibly the son of a schoolteacher:

> Why, even I—
> Born on the slopes of Pieria (the place
> Where Mnemosyne was nine times made a mother
> By Jove, the sire of the sisterhood of singers),
> Practically, I promise, in the precincts of a school,
>
> (3, Prologue, 18–21)

— That he came, or was brought, to Italy, probably when quite young. In the following lines the maxim quoted comes from one of the tragedies of Ennius, the father of Latin poetry, a work that may well have been part of a Roman education:

I intend to remember a maxim that I read
As a boy: "For a man of humble birth
It is not proper to protest in public."

(3, Epilogue, 44–46)

—That he suffered some sort of persecution at the hands of Sejanus, Tiberius' all-powerful minister:

Though some [of my fables] have got me into terrible
    trouble.
If my accuser, my judge, and my jury
Had been any other than simply Sejanus,
I'd have openly acknowledged my evident errors.

(3, Prologue, 45–48)

This passage also helps us with the dating: Sejanus died in A.D. 31, and thus Book 3 was evidently published after that date.
—That he was unpopular in certain intellectual circles, presumably because he was a foreigner by birth, an ex-slave, and successful:

If malign critics
Want to find fault, I'm quite indifferent—
They can criticize me to their hearts' content,
So long as they can't compete in my craft.

(4, Prologue, 19–22)

The reader will find a number of other expressions of the same sentiment.
—That he died in old age. This is surely a legitimate deduction from the last fable of his last book:

A dog who had once been dauntless and dashing
Against all wild game, and had given his master
Constant service and satisfaction,
Began to grow feeble from the burden of the years.
One day, doing battle with a bristling boar,
He had got it by the ear, but it easily escaped
By twisting away from the decayed teeth.

The hunter, deprived of his expected prey,
Scolded his hound, who then countered:
"It's strength, not spirit, that's deserted me, master.
If you want to blame me for what I've become,
You should give me credit for what I was."

(5, 10)

These are slim pickings, and of course there have been various attempts to deduce more. Critics who are supercilious about such attempts should remember what Phaedrus said in the second fable of his fourth book:

But even then I'd like you to look
Closely and carefully at these light-weight confections:
They conceal a lot of useful lessons.
They are not always exactly what they seem:
Outward appearances are often deceptive,
And few are favored with a fine enough sense
To discover what the artist has concealed in a corner.

The most ambitious reconstruction of Phaedrus' life and career has been made by an Italian scholar, Attilio de Lorenzi. He traces his whole life, from exposure by his mother at birth (see the strangely powerful fable "The Dog and the Lamb," 3, 15) at the door of a highly educated poet and teacher of Greek; his upbringing in the house of this cultivated man; his attachment to the retinue of L. Calpurnius Piso Frugi, who was given the task of settling disturbances in Thrace in the period 13–11 B.C.; his transfer, after Piso's return to Rome, to the house of Augustus as tutor to his grandson and joint heir, Lucius; his informal manumission;* his further transfer to the staff of Tiberius' villa at Cape Misenum near Naples, where he spent the rest of his life; his condemnation by Sejanus; and his eventual rehabilitation

---

* There were two levels of manumission, formal and informal. The formal kind involved a ceremony before a magistrate and conferred almost complete civil rights. The informal kind was effected by a statement of freedom by the master among friends, or a symbolic slap, or an invitation to sit at dinner with him. It did not confer full civil rights; e.g., it did not provide the freedom to start a business.

after Sejanus' death in A.D. 31. It is all done with constant reference to the history and mores of the times and with penetrating use of hints from the fables. No summary could do justice to the learning and ingenuity of this brilliant tour de force. However, intriguing as it is, very little of it unfortunately can be considered factual. What is solidly established is that by the time Phaedrus published his first book of fables he was a mature, assured, and accomplished artist, with a clear consciousness of his scope and his limitations. The first two fables, "The Wolf and the Lamb" and "The Frogs Ask for a King," are as concentrated, incisive, and effective as any that he wrote.

Phaedrus' surviving work consists of five books of fables (*fabellae*) based on the fables of Aesop, the traditional Greek inventor of the genre. There are thirty extra fables and three addresses to the reader in the so-called Perotti's Appendix,* whose quality is uneven and subject matter very varied but which are considered genuine and are included in the text of Perry, and in these translations. The five books are of unequal length, which is one reason for thinking that the collection as we have it is incomplete. They contain 31, 8, 19, 26 and 10 fables, respectively, with a prologue for each and epilogues for three. By no means all are animal fables: only 59 out of a total of 94 (75 out of 126, with Perotti's Appendix included).† The intermediary whom Phaedrus is thought to have used as the source for his work was the celebrated Athenian orator and statesman Demetrius of Phalerum, the contemporary and friend of the poet Menander who compiled, in prose, in the fourth century B.C., the only known collection before Phaedrus of Aesop's fables.‡

Phaedrus, Aesop, and the Problem of Folklore

Phaedrus is careful to tell us that his work is by no means mere imitation. In the first place, he has cast the fables in verse form:

---

* These were transcribed by the fifteenth-century scholar Niccoló Perotti from a manuscript of Phaedrus now lost.
† For contents of the fables, see below.
‡ The collection has not survived, but it is recorded by Diogenes Laertius (5, 80), author of a compendium of the lives and writings of the philosophers in the third century A.D.

Aesop is the author, the original inventor
Of the fables that follow, which I have refined
In a form of verse.

(1, Prologue, 1–3)

And then he develops the theme of independence much more fully in a later prologue:

Since, then, Particulo, you're partial to fables
(Which I call Aesopic, not actually Aesop's,
Since I've made more than the few he fathered,
Following his form, but with modern content),
You can now read the following, my fourth volume,

(4, Prologue, 14–18)

Phaedrus, then, thought that Aesop's fables had been invented and written by Aesop: he even tells us why, in the prologue to Book 3:

Slaves are exposed to incessant hazards.
Unable openly to express what he wanted,
One of them [Aesop] projected his personal opinions
Into fictional fables and found shelter
From carping critics in comic inventions.

This simple view of things, of course, was too good to last. Apart from the fact that Aesop was a semilegendary figure, a whole mass of conflicting theory has grown up in the area of myth and folklore, so much so in the case of fables that one critic has written: ". . . there is an 'Aesopic' just as there is a 'Homeric' Question." The question devolves from the same set of difficulties that puzzle students of myths and fairy tales. Iona and Peter Opie, for example, write: "Yet he [the student of fairy tales] finds himself faced by the astonishing fact that a body of tales have been found to be not merely ancient but to be traditional in a variety of countries and cultures, and that versions of a story told in widely separated parts of the earth will sometimes not merely bear resemblance, but possess actual points of detail in common."*

---

* Iona and Peter Opie, The Classic Fairy Tales, p. 21.

And Michael Grant, speaking of mythology: "Everyone who compares the Greek and Roman mythologies with those of other cultures throughout the various countries of the world, and throughout the successive periods of history, will be amazed, indeed staggered, by the frequency with which the same stories recur, in closely similar or identical form, in a vast number of different lands, times and contexts."[*]

And J. W. Duff on Phaedrus: "On the one hand, the well-springs lay far deeper in primeval Aryan tales than Phaedrus could have dreamed, and on the other hand the fables which he asumed to be by Aesop consisted largely of accretions subsequent to Aesop's time. The primitive beast story, so widespread an element in folklore, becomes literary when it is shaped either to satiric or moral purpose. Some such shaping of the beast fable lies at the root of the renown of the Samian slave, the actual 'Aisopos,' who flourished in the middle of the sixth century B.C. . . ."[†]

In very broad and oversimplified terms, the explanations offered for this phenomenon have been either psychological (that certain ideas and experiences are common and are likely to emerge anywhere at certain stages of development), morphological (that certain very general patterns of the structure of narrative are bound to recur), or diffusionist (that, improbable as it may sometimes seem, there is in fact some conduit of transmission between two or more similar, or even identical, but widely separated stories). Needless to say, no one of these theories alone has commanded general acceptance.[‡]

The Fables

To return to a more factual level, to the fables themselves as we have them and to what they contain and imply. Phaedrus' fables are

---

[*] Michael Grant and John Hazel, *Who's Who in Classical Mythology*, p. 8.

[†] J. Wight Duff, ed. A. M. Duff, *A Literary History of Rome in the Silver Age*, p. 110.

[‡] Anyone interested in pursuing this question in detail could usefully consult two learned articles on the duplication of the Phaedrus fable, Perotti's Appendix 16, "The Two Suitors": J. G. W. Henderson, "The Homing Instinct: A Folklore Theme in Phaedrus, App. Perott. 16 Perry/14 Postgate," *Proceedings of the Cambridge Philological Society*, new series 23 (1977): 17–31, and T. C. W. Stinton, "Phaedrus and Folklore: An

an amalgam of diverse elements. The great majority have in common a moral lesson, stated or implicit, namely, the animal fables and the overtly moral anecdotes. Besides these there are historical anecdotes, "King Demetrius and the Poet Menander" (5, 1); short stories, "The Widow and the Soldier"* (Perotti's Appendix 15); proverbs and sayings, "The Mountain in Labor" (4, 23); comic episodes, "The Butcher and the Monkey" (3, 4); curious facets of the behavior of animals, "The Hungry Bear" (Perotti's Appendix 22); and folk wisdom, "Aesop and the Farmer" (3, 3). And apart from their specific purposes, the fables shed incidental light on all sorts of interesting facets of Roman and Greek life: the status and level of expertise of doctors, women's attitude to childbearing, the cleverness and fair-mindedness of Augustus, pictures on tavern walls, variety acts in the theatre, and much else of random interest.

Phaedrus' attitude to life is one of dignified and humorous pessimism. There are the strong and there are the weak, and when it comes to a contest between the two, the stronger nearly always wins. The lamb, with justice and reason on his side, gets eaten by the wolf (1, 1); the cow, the she-goat, and the sheep imagine that they are equal partners with the lion, but, again in spite of justice and reason, when it comes to dividing up the spoils, the lion appropriates the whole lot (1, 5); the doves were stupid to put themselves under the protection of the kite (1, 31). And it is useless for the humble to protest. On the contrary, protesting may well bring a worse condition than the present one—as the frogs found when they asked for a more effective king than the log, and got sent a serpent (1, 2). And it was foolish of the crane to expect payment for removing a bone from the wolf's throat—it was payment enough that she was allowed to withdraw her head from his jaws (1, 8).

There is, however, a certain compensation for poverty: it offers no temptation to predators. The moral of "The Two Mules and the Robbers" is that poverty is safe and wealth is exposed to constant danger (2, 7). And there is one precious thing more important than all the

---

Old Problem Restated," *Classical Quarterly*, new series 29 (1979): 432–435. This latter article in particular is not only penetrating but also highly entertaining.

* This macabre story reappears as "The Widow of Ephesus" in Petronius' *Satyricon*, 111–112.

power and wealth in the world: freedom, as the wolf was clever enough to see when tempted by the dog to submit himself to a master (3, 7) and as the horse found when, in his attempt to get his revenge on the wild boar, he found himself subjected to a man (4, 4). Occasionally, the weak even have the satisfaction of seeing the strong paid out. The defrauded sheep has the pleasure of coming upon the wolf who gave false testimony against him lying dead in a pit (1, 17); the stork gets his own back on the fox by serving him, in return for his malicious joke, food that he cannot eat (1, 26); and the panther has his revenge on the humans who gratuitously maltreated him (3, 2).

Beyond all questions of power and weakness are lessons for everyone, the high and the lowly. Presumption and conceit are often punished. The jackdaw is banished by his peers for dressing himself up in the peacock's feathers (1, 3); the crow loses his cheese to the fox from vanity (1, 13); the frog bursts trying to make himself as big as the ox (1, 24); the fly makes himself ridiculous by his empty threats to the mule (3, 6); and the peacock is reproved by Juno for claiming more than has been allotted to him (3, 18).

Reputation

Phaedrus is usually classed in the literary histories among the "minor poets," but tribute has always been paid to his artful brevity (of which he himself was very proud, as we have seen above), his humor, and his simple and appropriate style and diction. He has been popular ever since his own day and has only been overshadowed in his chosen field in some respects by La Fontaine, who covered part of the same ground and acknowledged Phaedrus as one of his sources. Indeed, La Fontaine wrote in his preface to his fables:

> On ne trouvera pas ici l'élégance ni l'extrême brièveté qui rendent Phèdre recommandable: ce sont qualités au-dessus de ma portée. Comme il m'était impossible de l'imiter en cela, j'ai cru qu'il fallait en recompense égayer l'ouvrage plus qu'il n'a fait. Non que je le blâme d'en être demeuré dans ces termes; la langue latine n'en demandait pas davantage; et si l'on y veut prendre garde, on reconnaîtra dans cet auteur le vrai génie de Térence.

Neither the elegance nor the extreme brevity that are so appealing in Phaedrus will be found here: those are qualities beyond my scope. Since it was impossible for me to imitate him in that respect, I thought that I should make up for it by enlivening the work more than he had done. Not that I find fault with him for having stayed within those limits; the Latin language required no more; and if you pay close attention, you will find in this author the true genius of Terence.

Generous words. And all the more so, in that it is precisely because of his ability to "enliven" (*égayer*), which includes the delicate characterization of his creatures and the easy appropriateness of his rhyming, that La Fontaine is so much admired.

Phaedrus had another claim to fame in his day: to have been the first to adapt a whole Greek genre to Latin literature. In the Roman literary context this was an important contribution. Latin writers felt overshadowed by the vast achievement of Greece in so many areas of literature, and any writer who pioneered in introducing one of them to the Roman public was proud of his feat and was entitled to consider that he had done something original. Thus Virgil's model for the Eclogues was the Sicilian Greek Theocritus (cf. Eclogue 4, 1); for the Georgics, Hesiod (cf. Georgics, 2, 176), and for his epic poem, Homer. In fact the only genre in which Latin writing did not start from a Greek model was satire: hence the celebrated claim by the rhetorician and critic Quintilian, "Satire is entirely ours."

Thus, the position of an innovator like Phaedrus was ambiguous. He was proud of introducing something that was admittedly not entirely his; and he was equally proud of having to some extent transcended his model and made the material his own. He writes in the prologue to Book 2:

> When I elaborate the incidents of a story,
> If it catches the ear and adds color to the content,
> My efforts should be appreciated on their own merits
> And not go unnoticed under the name of Aesop.
> Of course, I shall be careful to conserve his spirit;
> But if I indulge in inventions of my own,

To divert my public by the pleasure of variety,
I count on you, Reader, for your kind indulgence,
And may conciseness compensate for the license you
    allow me.

(2, Prologue, 5–13)

And later in the same book:

Forestalled by another from being first in the field,
I have labored long at the little that was left me,
Namely to ensure that he should not be unique;
And not out of envy, but emulation.
And if my efforts find favor with Rome,
She'll have one more weapon to wield in the challenge
Against Greece; and if green-eyed
Jealousy pleases to disparage my pains,
She will not steal from me my self-esteem.

(2, 9, 5–13)

Meter of Translation

Phaedrus wrote in the meter of Iambic Senarii, that is, lines of six iambic feet, with various resolutions and variations. This was one of the standard meters used for dialogue and soliloquy in Greek and Roman drama and, as such, was well suited to Phaedrus' style and purpose. Unfortunately, in English, whereas the *five-foot* iambic line is a natural verse rhythm for English speech, the *six-foot* iambic line has never taken hold, and for some mysterious psychometrical reason it reads awkwardly. I have chosen to express Phaedrus' fluent and colloquial rhythms in a modified version of Anglo-Saxon and Middle English alliterative verse, as exemplified by *Piers Plowman* and revived by W. H. Auden (successfully, as I think) in *The Age of Anxiety*. The meter is simple. It consists of unrhymed lines of no fixed number of syllables, but with four stresses in each line, each line being divided into two halves with two stresses each. In its pure form, at least two, usually three, and occasionally four of the stressed words are alliterated, the alliteration being set by the first stressed word of the second half, that is, the third beat. Thus, *Piers Plowman* begins:

In a súmmer séason when sóft was the sún

and *The Age of Anxiety:*

My déuce, my dóuble, my déar ímage

And my version of Phaedrus 1, 1:

To the sélfsame stréam, to sláke their thírst

I have allowed myself considerable latitude in the matter of alliteration, preferring to depart from strict orthodoxy rather than from
the required sense. I have not always based the alliteration on the
third stress; I have used assonance of vowels sometimes in place of
alliteration of consonants; I have sometimes used two different allit-
erations in one line; and there are some lines with little or no alliteration, but in that case usually referring alliteratively to the line before
or after. Given this freedom, it is a natural meter to write, congenial
to English speech, and, I think, easy to read. I hope that the reader
finds it so.

Christopher Smart's Translation

The last translation of Phaedrus into English verse was made by
Christopher Smart and was published in 1764.* Smart had been confined in Potter's madhouse in Bethnal Green for the four years between 1759 and early 1763. Soon after his release he published a volume of poems, A *Song to David*, and a translation of the Psalms into

---

* It is accessible in the Bohn series of classical translations in the volume entitled "The
Comedies of Terence and the Fables of Phaedrus, literally translated into English
prose with notes, by Henry Thomas Riley, B.A., to which is added A *Metrical Translation of Phaedrus* by Christopher Smart, A.M. London, Bell and Daldy, 1872." There is
also a version by Sir Brooke Boothby, Bart (Edinburgh: Archibald Constable and Co.,
1809) concealed under the title *Fables and Satires*. Besides Phaedrus, it contains fables
from various other sources, including some of La Fontaine's, and four satires of his
own. It is similar in style and meter to Smart's translations and is often neat and
trenchant in expression, but it sacrifices so much to brevity and the demands of
rhyme as to be closer to a paraphrase than a translation.

rhyming verse. He had also been writing the extraordinary *Jubilate Agno*, although this was not published in his lifetime, or indeed until 1939. This output is proof of the limited nature of his madness. He was afflicted (if that is the word) with a religious mania that manifested itself in the constant desire to pray and, when in public places, to draw others into prayer with him; but it is clear that his intellect was not affected. In December 1764 he published his translation of Phaedrus, and it seems probable that he had been working on that also during his time in the madhouse.

Smart's translation is in eight-syllable rhyming couplets. It was addressed primarily to a young audience (and a Latin-learning one at that) and was dedicated to the sons of some patrons of his. In an advertisement for it he wrote: "Upon the whole, the young reader by this explanatory version and parsing index will get the drift of the author's meaning, learn his syntax, and make a better progress in the tongue than he would by a mere prose translation, which is rather too great a help."* Smart was a good scholar. He had been a fellow of Pembroke College, Cambridge, and was proud of his reputation as a classicist. The review in the *Critical Review* concluded: "Phaedrus is remarkably concise; this version is diffuse. In some places the translator has embellished the author's narration, and given an ingenious turn to a simple expression: but he has not refined his language with a proper degree of nicety and care; many of his verses are encumbered with feeble expletives and unnecessary words."

In general, this is a reasonable criticism. But in fairness to Smart it should be said, first, that it is impossible in an extended translation to match the conciseness of Latin in English owing to the difference in grammar and syntax of the two languages; second, that the intrusion of unnecessary words is a feature endemic to rhymed translation, a form the fashion of the eighteenth century almost dictated (Smart's rhyming, at which he had had long practice in his work on the Psalms, quite apart from his own poems, was admirably versatile and deft); and third, that the famous conciseness of Phaedrus is not always a virtue, but could sometimes rather be called sparseness.

---

* I am indebted for this and other information about Smart to *Christopher Smart, Scholar of the University* by Arthur Sherbo.

Here is a good specimen of Smart's manner in a familiar fable (Phaedrus 4, 3):

The Fox and the Grapes

An hungry fox with fierce attack
Sprang on a vine, but tumbled back,
Nor could attain the point in view,
So near the sky the bunches grew.
5   As he went off, "They're scurvy stuff,"
Says he, "and not half ripe enough—
And I've more reverence for my tripes
Than to torment them with the gripes."
      For those this tale is very pat
10   Who lessen what they can't come at.

Phaedrus' original displays his conciseness at its best, and Smart, with a few omissions, comes close to it: only the seventh and eighth lines could be regarded as unduly expanded.

BIBLIOGRAPHY

Currie, H. MacL. "Phaedrus the Fabulist." In *Aufstieg und Niedergang der Römischen Welt*, ed. Hildegard Temporini and Wolfgang Haase, 32.1, 497–513. Berlin: Walter de Gruyter, 1985.

De Lorenzi, Attilio. *Fedro*. Florence: La Nuova Italia, 1955.

Duff, J. Wight. "Phaedrus and the Fable." In *A Literary History of Rome in the Silver Age*, ed. A. M. Duff, 107–123. 2 ed. London: Ernest Benn, 1960.

Goodyear, F. R. D. "Phaedrus." In *The Cambridge History of Classical Literature*, ed. P. E. Easterling and E. J. Kenney, part II, Roman Literature, 624–626. Cambridge: Cambridge University Press, 1982.

Grant, Michael, and John Hazel. *Who's Who in Classical Mythology*. London: Weidenfeld and Nicolson, 1973.

Opie, Iona and Peter. *The Classic Fairy Tales*. New York: Oxford University Press, 1980.

Perry, B. E., trans. *Babrius and Phaedrus*. Loeb Classical Library. Cambridge, Mass. and London: Harvard University Press and William Heinemann, 1965, repr. 1975.

Thompson, Stith. *Motif-Index of Folk-Literature*. Bloomington and London: Indiana University Press, 1955–1958 and reprinted.

BOOK 1

The text, with apparatus criticus, used for this translation is that of J. P. Postgate in his *Corpus Poetarum Latinorum*, Vol. 2 (London: Bell and Sons, 1905), with occasional correction and assistance from B. E. Perry's text in his edition of *Babrius and Phaedrus* in the Loeb Classical Library.

PROLOGUE

Aesop is the author, the original inventor
Of the fables that follow, which I have refined
In the form of verse.* This modest volume
Has a twofold attraction: it entertains
And gives careful counsel for the conduct of life.
If anyone chooses to carp and complain
That trees are speaking,† not to mention beasts,
My answer is that I aim to amuse.
What follow are fables fabricated in fun.

---

* Literally, *in the metre of senarii*. The whole of Phaedrus' fables are written in this meter. Each line is composed of six iambic or spondaic feet, with a number of permitted variations and resolutions. The basic rhythm is iambic. Thus, the first two lines run:
Āesṓ|pŭs āŭc|tōr qūǎm | mātérī|ǎm rép|pěrít
hānc égo | pŏlí|vī vér|sĭbús | sĕnä́|rĭís.
† In the fables as we have them, no trees speak. We can only assume that the reference is to other fables now lost.

Illustrations in this edition are from
the facsimile edition of the German Esopus,
Ernst Voulliéme, Augsburg, 1477.

1. THE WOLF AND THE LAMB

To the selfsame stream, to slake their thirst,
Came a wolf and a lamb. The wolf was standing
Upstream, and the lamb a long way lower.
The ruthless predator, provoked by the prompting
Of his greedy gullet, invented grounds
For an altercation. "What," he accused,
"Do you mean by making my water muddy?"
"Wolf," the woolly one warily answered,
"How can I be the cause of your discomfort?
The water descends in a downward direction
From you to me." The wolf, refuted
By the sheer rigor of reason, replied,
"So, six months ago you meanly maligned me."
"But that," said the lamb, "was before I was born."
"Then it must be your father who meanly maligned me."
And he pounced on his prey and tore him to pieces,
Indifferent to all equity and justice.

This fable is fashioned to fit those oppressors
Who trump up pretexts to entrap the innocent.

2. THE FROGS ASK FOR A KING

When all at Athens enjoyed equality
Under law, liberty exceeded due limits*
And carried the state near collapse and chaos.
This led to factions, feuds, and confederacies,
Until finally a tyrant took total control.
This was Pisistratus. Soon the people proceeded
To chafe at the checks on their cherished freedom:
Not that the repression was especially savage,
But because all unusual burdens are unbearable.
When the commons were complaining, the occasion prompted
Aesop to elaborate an appropriate fable:

When the frogs were freely frolicking in the marshes,
The conservative element came to the conclusion
That the freedom they had fostered had gone too far,
So they cried out to Jupiter to consign them a king
Who would curb these excesses and decadence by force.
The Supreme Deity smiled, and sent them
A small log of wood, which he lobbed down to land there
With a sudden splash, whose sound and disturbance
Threw the timid tribe into a state of terror.
Then it lay there, mutely merged in the mud,
Until one frog warily emerged from the surface
And stealthily explored the sovereign that was sent them,
Then called to his comrades, who came out with a clamor
And, observing that the object was only a timber,
Jubilantly jumped and romped on its back,
Insulting it with every imaginable indignity.

---

* This probably refers to the period when Solon was appointed Archon in 594–593
B.C. His reforms freed the people from serfdom and the burden of debt and established the constitution of Athens. His institutions remained as the basis of the future democracy developed by Cleisthenes in the fifth century. Nevertheless, in 560
Pisistratus made himself tyrant. After two periods of exile he maintained control of
Athens from 546 until his death in 527. His tyranny appears, in fact, to have been
rather benevolent, as is suggested by the eighth line of this fable.

They applied again for another king,
Since the kind that had come was completely useless.
Jove sent them a snake, whose sharp teeth
Began to grab and gobble them one by one.
The frogs sat there stunned. Their power of speech
Failed them, their efforts to escape were futile.
They managed to smuggle a message through Mercury
To Jupiter, pleading for pity in their plight.
The only answer from the Thunderer was this:
"You were grudging and ungrateful when I gave you the good:
So put up with the present, bad as it may be."

And Aesop added: "You also, Athenians,
Accept this servitude, in spite of its severity,
Or you well may fall into one that is worse."

3. THE PRESUMPTUOUS JACKDAW AND THE PEACOCK

To aspire to accomplishments allotted to others
Instead of being satisfied with your solid endowments
In the normal manner that Nature intended
Is foolish—as is found in the following fable.

Swollen with self-importance, a stupid jackdaw
Put on some feathers that had fallen from a peacock
And insinuated himself into the select circle
Of those brilliant birds, abandoning his brothers
As beneath his notice. In no time the nincompoop
Paid for his presumption by being stripped of his plumage
And banished by their beaks. Then, badly battered,
The jackdaw in dejection returned to his tribe,
Or tried to, but met with more humiliation,
Rejected, and lectured by a moralist among them:
"If you had stayed in the station assigned to you,
Accepting what Nature in her wisdom wanted,
You'd have been uninjured—no insults from those others,
And no ignominious expulsion from your own."

4. THE DOG CARRYING A PIECE OF MEAT ACROSS A RIVER

A person who pursues the property of another
Is likely to lose what belonged to himself,
And deservedly so.
                              A marauding dog
With a stolen morsel of meat in his mouth
Was carrying it across a calm river.
Suddenly, as he swam along, he spotted
His own image in the waveless water
Perfectly reproduced. Presuming it another
Meal in the mouth of a different dog,
He planned to purloin it, but was disappointed.
In his grasping greed he let go his gobbet,
And failed to fasten on the prize that he fancied.

5. THE COW, THE SHE-GOAT, THE SHEEP, AND THE LION

Partnership with the powerful is always precarious,
As the fable that follows poignantly displays.

A cow, a she-goat, and a long-suffering sheep
Were co-partners with a lion in a copse in the country.
One day, when they'd captured a colossal stag,
The lion divided it and addressed them all:
"I am called lion, so I claim the first quarter;
My share as associate secures me the second;
I am certainly the strongest, so I seize the third;
And you put a paw on the fourth at your peril."
Thus bare-faced bullying brought the lion the lot.

6. THE FROGS COMPLAIN ABOUT THE SUN

For the nuptials of his next-door neighbor, a thief,
Aesop invented the following anecdote:

When the sun once decided to select a wife,
The frogs filled the firmament with a fearful uproar.
Jupiter, disturbed by the din, desired
To know the cause of their clamorous complaint.
One of the people of the pond explained:
"While there's only one of him, he sucks away our water,
So we languish and die for lack of liquid.
What future have we if he fathers a family?"

7. THE FOX AND THE TRAGIC ACTOR'S MASK

A fox-philosopher came across
The majestic mask of a tragic actor.
"What a splendid façade," he said to himself,
"And never a bit of brains behind it."

This allegory is aimed at those dolts and dummies
Whom fortune has loaded with fame and favors,
But left bereft of sound sense.

8. THE WOLF AND THE CRANE

If you reckon on a reward for services rendered
From scoundrels, you're a dupe and doubly deluded:
You're aiding dastards who don't deserve it;
And you've little likelihood of escaping unscathed.

There was once a wolf who had swallowed a bone,
Which stuck in his throat, and he suffered so severely
That he went round his neighbors one by one
Promising to pay them if they'd pull it out.
In the end the only animal to agree
Was the crane. Won over by an oath on his honor,
She lunged into his gullet with her long neck
And successfully performed the perilous operation.
But when it came to her claiming the payment,
The other answered, "You ungrateful creature!
I had your head helpless in my mouth
And let you withdraw it—and you want a reward!"

9. THE SPARROW GIVES ADVICE TO THE HARE

To place yourself in peril while preaching precaution
Is stupid, as this simple story will show you.

Caught in an eagle's clutches, and crying
Pitifully, a hare was spotted by a sparrow,
Who sneered sarcastically, "That speed that you boast of,
Where has it landed you? Were your legs too lazy?"
But in mid-harangue he was hoisted by a hawk,
Who was deaf to his protests and duly dispatched him.
The hare, still half-alive, was heard
To gasp in his agony, "Well, you've given me something,
Some comfort to console me as I quit the scene.
A moment ago you were mocking my misfortune,
In safety yourself: now you're singing the same
Lament as I did on leaving this life."

10. THE WOLF AND THE FOX RECEIVE JUDGMENT FROM THE APE

People with a reputation for persistent deceit
Aren't trusted even when they're telling the truth:
As is found exemplified by this fable of Aesop's.

A wolf was lodging a charge of larceny
Against a fox, who growled, "Not guilty."
Then a monkey intervened, and made himself magistrate
To decide between them. When they'd done with declaiming,
The simian is said to have pronounced this sentence:
"Wolf, you didn't 'lose' the property that you plead for;
And fox, you did steal what you indignantly deny." *

---

* The implication is that the wolf had stolen the property in the first place and so
could not be said to have lost what was not really his.

11. THE LION AND THE ASS GO HUNTING

The man of mean spirit who bullies and brags,
Proclaiming his courage, may convince newcomers,
But is only a figure of fun to his familiars.

A lion enlisted as colleague for the hunt
An ass, whom he hid in a thicket, with instructions
To alarm the animals with his bugle-like bray
(All the more horrible because they hadn't heard it),
While he would catch them as they came from their cover.
Long-ears filled his lungs and bellowed his loudest
And bewildered the beasts by the novelty of the noise.
Hurrying through their habitual holes of escape
In alarm and amazement, they emerged in the open,
To be met and massacred and mangled by the lion.
Exhausted by the slaughter, he called to his ally
To cut off the accompaniment. The conceited creature
Cried, "Weren't you pretty impressed by my vocal
    performance?"
"Marvelous," said the lion. "So much so, I admit,
That unless I had known your negligible nature
And what a great ass you actually are,
I too would have taken to my heels in terror."

12. THE STAG AT THE FOUNTAIN

The assets you disparage will do duty sometimes
Better than more prized blessings. As below.

A stag, after drinking at a spring, stood still,
Amazed at his image mirrored in the water.
He admired extravagantly his branching antlers,
But the thinness of his legs he thought pathetic.
Then, suddenly startled by the shouts of hunters,
He took to his heels in hot haste
And outdistanced the dogs in pursuit on the plain.
But when he came to the close cover
Of a forest, he found that his progress was impeded
By his horns entwined in the tangle of the thicket.
Then the pack pounced on him and tore him to pieces.
As he breathed his last, he bequeathed this lesson:
"What a sad denouement—I never knew
What a blessing would be the gifts that I belittled,
And what pain was in store from the parts that I praised."

13. THE FOX AND THE CROW

To respond with pleasure to flattering approaches
Leads to retribution, ridicule, and regret.

A crow was ensconced in a tall tree,
Holding in his beak a bit of cheese
Which he'd pertly purloined from an open window,
When a fox spied him and schemed how to steal it,
And proceeded to speak slyly as follows:
"My good crow, what gloss and glamour
Your feathers have—what a fine face—
What beauty in your whole body and bearing!
If only your song had a sweeter sound,
Not a bird in the country could compare with your charms."
The conceited creature, anxious to excel
In virtue of voice as in all else,
Opened up his beak and began to bellow,
And so let fall his food, which the cunning fox
Snapped up from the ground and swallowed in a second.
Too late the crow had learned his lesson:
He wailed woefully and went without.

14. FROM COBBLER TO PHYSICIAN

An incompetent cobbler, completely penniless,
Set up as a doctor in a different district.
By peddling some pills that he passed off as an "antidote"
He had built up a business, with brazen advertising.
This character was called in by the king of the city
When one of his ministers lay mortally ill.
To test the man's technical talent and integrity,
He called for a cup, in which he crushed the antidote;
He then poured in water, pretending it was poison,
And handed it to our hero to drink up himself.
Trembling with fear, the fellow confessed
That his fame as a physician was founded not
On any knowledge of his art, but only
On the pitiful credulity of the impressionable public.
The king summoned his assembly and spoke as follows:
"People of mine, you must be mad
If you blithely deliver your lives to a fellow
Who was shunned as unfit to put shoes on your feet."

This story could serve as a sermon for those
Whose ignorance provides an income for imposters.

15. WHAT THE ASS SAID TO THE OLD SHEPHERD

Revolutions, reversals of regimes and rulers,
For the moneyless masses mean a change of masters,
No more. I'll tell you a tale in illustration.

An old shepherd, nervous by nature,
Watched his ass feeding in a flowery field.
All of a sudden the shouts of soldiers
Broke in on the browsing. Bewildered and frightened,
The old man urged his ass to escape.
Asses are slow and supposed to be stupid,
But this one countered with a clever question:
"Tell me something. Suppose that these soldiers
Take me as loot: are they likely to load me
With my present packsaddle plus another?"
"Can't be done," said the dotard. "What difference, then,
Does it make to me what man is my master,
If I'm still only burdened with a single saddle?"

16. THE SHEEP, THE STAG, AND THE WOLF

When a swindler gets scoundrels to support a contract,
He's not bringing you business, but building up trouble.

A stag asked a sheep for the loan of a sack
Of wheat, for which the wolf would be summoned
To stand as surety. But the sheep was mistrustful:
"The wolf's policy is to plunder and depart—
And you yourself are used to escaping
At lightning speed. Where, please, shall I look for you
When the day of repayment duly dawns?"

17. THE SHEEP, THE DOG, AND THE WOLF

Liars are liable to lose in the end.

One day a dog was demanding recompense
For a loaf of bread, which he lyingly alleged
He'd entrusted to a sheep to take care of for a time.
He summoned as witness a wolf, who swore
That the items taken were ten, not just one.
The sheep was condemned on this crooked charge
And forced unfairly to fork out.
A few days later, she lighted on the wolf
Lying dead in a pit, and declared to herself:
"Well, well; so these are the wages of the wicked
That the powers above have paid him for his perjury."

18. A WOMAN IN CHILDBIRTH

One is wary of a place that was productive of pain.

A woman, having passed through her pregnancy, on the point
Of giving birth, lay groaning on the ground.
When her husband begged her to bear the baby
More decently on the bed, and with less discomfort,
She countered, "You expect me to trust that my troubles
Will cease in the same spot where they started?"

19. THE DOG AND HER LITTER OF PUPPIES

The reasonable-sounding requests of rogues
Are smooth on the surface but conceal a trap,
As the following verses vividly evince.

A dog, on the point of producing some puppies,
Asked permission from a friend to deposit her litter
In the other's kennel. She kindly consented.
When the owner asked for her home back,
The intruder begged for a brief reprieve—
Long enough, at least, for her little ones
To grow sufficiently strong to take safely away.
That time also elapsed, and the owner
Redoubled her demands for her domicile.
"Convince me," the creature callously countered,
"That you're a match for me and my brood, and I'll move."

20. THE HUNGRY DOGS

An impractical project is doubly dangerous:
It is ineffective, and it draws men to destruction.

Some dogs spotted something on the surface of a river—
A hide, half-sunk. To haul it ashore
More easily and eat it, they evolved a scheme:
To drain the river. So they got down to drinking,
And drank and drank until they burst and died
Before their greed could get to its goal.

21. THE OLD LION, THE BOAR, THE BULL, AND THE ASS

A person deprived of his dignity, and reduced
From fame to affliction, can find himself exposed
To insults and ignominy from the lowest of the low.

A lion, old, enervated, and exhausted,
Lying listless in his last extremity,
Was beset by a boar, who with terrible tusks
Viciously avenged an old grievance.
Then a bull brutally gored with his horns
His ancient antagonist. An ass, who meanwhile
Had seen the weakened creature maltreated
Without counterattacking, gave a crashing kick
Full in his face. And he faintly lamented
With his dying breath, "To be bullied by the brave
Was bad enough, but when you abuse me,
You disgrace to nature, and I'm made to take it—
Then I seem to be dying a double death."

22. THE WEASEL AND THE MAN

A weasel, manoeuvred by a man into a trap,
Eager at all costs to avoid death,
Pleaded pitifully, "Spare me, please.
Thanks to me, not a murmur of mice,
Those horrible creatures, is heard in your house."
The man answered, "If in fact you were acting
In my interests, you'd be giving me grounds
To thank you, and I'd happily have answered your appeal.
But I'm well aware that what you want
Is to swallow these succulent scraps that marauding
Mice would make meals of, and then the mice themselves:
So don't go setting me down as your debtor
For a good turn that you never intended."
And he snuffed out the sly thing's life instanter.

This moral story is meant to mirror
People who promote their personal advancement
While bragging of the boons that their so-called benevolence
Has supposedly conferred on the credulous crowd.

23. THE FAITHFUL DOG

A sudden access of unexpected kindness
May catch the fancy of fools but is futile
When it tries to entrap intelligent subjects.

A thief in the night threw down some bread,
Designed to deceive a dog on the watch.
"Aha! Trying to stop my tongue,"
Said the dog, "and prevent me from doing my duty
By barking a warning? You're badly mistaken.
On the contrary, such uncommon kindness
Is an extra incitement to staying alert.
You won't break in by bamboozling me:
This watchdog won't help you on the way to wealth."

24. THE FROG WHO BURST HIMSELF AND THE BULL

When the poor presume to copy the powerful
In rancorous rivalry, the result is ruin.

There once was a frog frolicking in a field
Where a bull nearby was bulkily browsing.
Seized with jealousy of its sensational size,
He sat himself down and summoned up his strength
And puffed and puffed until he'd fully inflated
His wrinkled skin, then called to his comrades,
"Am I now bigger than that beastly bull?"
When they answered "No," with another enormous
Effort he filled his frame even fuller
And asked them again, and again the answer
Was "No." So, baffled and belligerent, he blew
And blew and blew and blew until he burst.

25. THE DOGS AND THE CROCODILES

Those who give crooked counsel to the cautious
Are wasting their breath, and besides that
They receive in response only ridicule and rejection.

When dogs in the Delta want to drink from the Nile,
They do it, so rumor reports, on the run—
A precaution against being caught by crocodiles.*
Well, when one of these dogs took a running drink,
A crocodile called out, "Take your time,
Lap it up at your leisure, this lovely water,
And don't be frightened!" But the dog, no dupe,
Retorted, "I'd certainly savor it slowly,
I would indeed, if I weren't aware
How eager you are to eat me for your dinner."

---

* This is recorded by Pliny, *Natural History*, 8, 40.

26. THE FOX AND THE STORK

Be unkind to no man: and never forget
That mean behavior is liable to rebound,
As the following fable graphically forewarns.

A fox once summoned a stork to supper
And served her some soup in a shallow dish,
Which of course the bird was quite incapable,
For all her appetite, of eating at all.
So she asked him back and brought before him
Some nice minced food in a narrow-necked
Porcelain pot, in which she put her beak
And gobbled greedily, while her hungry guest
Brooded baffled—the best he could do
Was uselessly lick at the vessel's neck.
And the stork said, "If you start playing tricks,
You must put up patiently with being paid back."

27. THE DOG, THE TREASURE, AND THE VULTURE

This story has a moral for misers and for men
Base born, but bent on being reckoned rich.

A dog, while digging up the buried bones
Of a human skeleton, hit on a treasure,
And, since he had desecrated the spirits of the dead,
He was cursed with a maniacal thirst for money—
A proper penalty paid for his impiety.
So, in guarding the gold he forgot about food
And starved to death. A visiting vulture
Stopped by his body and is supposed to have said:
"Quite right, dog. You deserved this death,
Since you suddenly reached out for royal riches
Though conceived in the gutter and suckled in a sewer."

28. THE FOX AND THE EAGLE

It is good policy for the great and grand
To treat their lessers with respect. Revenge
Is available to all, regardless of rank,
And you never know who may prove to be clever.

An eagle carried off the cubs of a fox
And set them in her nest as food for her fledglings.
The mother fox frantically followed
And begged the brigand not to bring her
Such a load of affliction as the loss of her little ones.
Safe in the stronghold of her eyrie, the eagle
Ignored her cries with callous contempt.
The fox then snatched a flaming firebrand
From a nearby altar and in no time at all
Set a circle of fire on the forest floor
Round the tall tree, and thereby threatened
Fatality to the family of her feathered foe.
To deliver her young from the danger of death,
The eagle reversed the roles: she resorted
To supplication to ensure their safety,
And carried back the cubs to the care of the fox.

29. THE ASS INSULTS THE BOAR

Idiots angling for an easy laugh
Often inflict insults on others
And thereby threaten themselves with danger.

An ass met a boar and brayed out, "Brother,
Good morning." The boar was aggrieved at the greeting
And asked the ass to account for his insult.
The ass protruded his pizzle and persisted,
"If you contend we have nothing in common,
I assure you that *this* is similar to your snout."
The boar was about to make a battering attack,
As he would on another of nobler nature,
But managed to control his choler and muttered,
"Revenge would be easy, but I refuse
To besmirch myself with such base-born blood."

30. THE FROGS AFRAID OF THE BATTLE OF THE BULLS

When high-ups quarrel, the humble get hurt.

A battle was in progress between two bulls,
When a frog, emerging from the mire of his marsh
Some way away, watched them and warned his fellows:
"Oh, dear, we're threatened with a dreadful disaster."
When asked by the others to explain his anxiety,
Since the bulls were battling for the headship of the herd
And lived their lives on land that was firm,
Far off from the treacherous fen of the frogs,
The sage expatiated: "What you say is sensible.
Their domain is dry land, I don't deny it,
And bulls as a breed don't bother with us;
But when two contend for control of the meadows,
The beaten bull will betake himself here,
Heading for our haven as a hiding place,
And batter us to bits with his hard hooves.
So we are affected by their furious feuding."

31. THE KITE AND THE DOVES

When you need help, if you hope to have it
On the warranty of the wicked, you're wasting your time:
From such you're doomed to death and disaster.

A kite kept constant and careful watch
Intending to dispatch some doves to their death.
When the speed of their wings consistently saved them,
The predator pondered a plan of entrapment
And wooed his victims with these wily words:
"Your lives are beset by incessant anxiety.
Why not come to terms and create me your king,
To protect and preserve you from all possible harm?"
The doves, not doubting him, did as he suggested.
But no sooner had the kite acquired his kingship
Than he started to swoop on them with his savage claws,
And dove by dove they were duly devoured,
Mercilessly mangled in his majesty's maw.
Then sighed a subject who was still surviving,
"Deservedly does the doom of death await us,
For letting this brigand be lord of our lives."

BOOK 2

AUTHOR'S PROLOGUE

The art of Aesop is essentially moral.
The primary point and purpose of his fables
Is to make manifest and amend the mistakes of mortals
And so to sharpen their self-awareness.
When I elaborate the incidents of a story,
If it catches the ear and adds color to the content,
My efforts should be appreciated on their own merits
And not go unnoticed under the name of Aesop.
Of course, I shall be careful to conserve his spirit;
But if I indulge in inventions of my own,
To divert my public by the pleasure of variety,
I count on you, Reader, for your kind indulgence,
And may conciseness compensate for the license you allow me.
But before my pride in my brevity becomes boring,
Let me give some advice. Be grudging to the greedy,
But offer the modest even more than they've asked for.

1. THE BULLOCK, THE LION, AND THE BANDIT

A lion was standing astride a bullock
He had just bagged, when a bandit came by
And, seeing it, requested a share of the spoil.
"I'd let you have it," said the lion, "unless
I'd heard of your habit of helping yourself
To people's possessions without their permission,"
And rebuffed the robber. There arrived at this moment
An innocent traveler, who retraced his steps
At the sight of the lion; but the latter allayed
His fear and bellowed benignly, "Be brave!
Your modest manner has merited a portion—
Have the courage to take it." And he carved up the carcass
And withdrew to the woods, with the wayfarer
Given free access to the fabulous find.

A laudable and uplifting lesson, no doubt:
But in grim reality the greedy gain,
And meek manners get a meager return.

2. TWO WOMEN, ONE OLD, ONE YOUNG, IN LOVE WITH THE SAME MAN

One way or another, women always win,
And men are likely, whether loving or loved,
To be reduced to destitution: as in the anecdotes.

A mature, well-preserved woman was worried
About how to keep her hold on a middle-aged man;
While a younger in years had him yearning for her.
The two of them, determined to transform him appropriately,
Proceeded, in turn, to pull hairs from his head.
The subject, supposing he was being spruced up
By the constant care of the two charming creatures,
Became suddenly bald: for the younger beauty,
To keep his age at bay, banished all the white,
While the elder, to suppress the excess of youthfulness,
Had ruthlessly uprooted the betraying black.

3. AESOP'S WORDS TO A MAN
ABOUT THE SUCCESS OF WRONGDOERS

A citizen bitten by a vicious dog
Dipped a bit of bread in his own blood
And hurled it at the culprit, having heard
That that was the cure for this category of wound.
Then Aesop pleaded, "Please, I implore you,
Don't be seen doing this by any more dogs.
Otherwise they'll eat us all alive
When they see that skull duggery is so rewarding."

When crooks can count on an easy coup,
Others are encouraged to act likewise.

4. THE EAGLE, THE CAT, AND THE WILD BOAR

An eagle had its eyrie high in an oak;
A cat found a hollow half-way up
To bear its kittens in; and at the base a wild boar
Had laid its litter. Soon this chance community
Was totally overturned and destroyed
By the blackguardly machinations of the cat.
First she climbed up to the eagle's eyrie
And cried, "Catastrophe's coming to us both!
All that excavation every day—
You've seen it yourself—that beastly boar
Is intending to overturn the oak,
Get our children to the ground, and gobble them up."
Having bred dismay and bewildered the bird,
She crept down to the abode of the bristly boar
And hissed, "Something horrible will happen to your young,
For as soon as your family fares forth to forage
That eagle will pounce and pluck away your piglets."
So, having succeeded in sowing terror
There, too, our trickster retired
And hid in the hollow where she had her home.
Then at night she silently stalked out,
Supplied her family with sufficient food,
Then all day long lay low
Feigning fear, but actually on the alert.
The eagle, expecting the end any second,
Sat there still in the branches, while the boar,
Afraid for her litter, never left her lair.
So eagle and boar and both their broods
(To cut a long story short) soon starved
And thereby provided, as planned, a plentiful
Feast for the kittens of the crafty cat.

This fable offers an object lesson
To credulous, careless, and foolish folk
In how much damage a double-dealing,
Cunning character is capable of causing.

5. TIBERIUS' WORDS TO AN ATTENDANT

Social climbers and self-servers,
Full of fawning and officious fussiness,
Always on the go—we know them in Rome:
Bustling about and busy with nothings,
Not even profiting from their own exertions,
A plague on the public and pernicious to themselves.
I hope to help rehabilitate and reform them
By a true anecdote that deserves attention.

Tiberius once, on his way to Naples,
Stopped at his country estate at Misenum.*
Perched on a promontory, placed there by Lucullus,†
It surveyed both Sicilian and Tuscan seas.
A minor member of the mansion's staff,
A natty fellow with a neat fringe
On his fashionable frock coat of Egyptian linen,
While his master was going round the glorious garden,
Started to water the parched path
With a wooden pot, in a pretentious display
Of efficient performance of his flunkey's duties.
The reaction? Ridicule. But unrebuffed
He rushed ahead to another area
And continued assiduously suppressing the dust.
Tiberius recognized him, realized the reason
For this unsolicited, excessive energy,
Knew what he hoped for, and hailed him, "Hey!"
Instant reaction: the man dashed up,
Confidently expecting a tremendous tip.
But that day His Majesty was in a mocking mood:
"What you've done is nothing, and nothing will come of it.
It costs more than that to get a slap from me."‡

---

* Cape Misenum was at the tip of the northern arm of the Bay of Naples.
† Consul in 74 B.C., Lucullus was given command of an army against Mithridates, King of Pontus on the Black Sea. He conducted a long series of campaigns in Asia Minor and was eventually superseded by Pompey. It was then that he indulged in the taste for luxury and extravagance with which his name is associated.
‡ A symbolic slap was the formal gesture made by a master when granting freedom to a slave, and the word *alapa*, a slap, is used here and elsewhere to denote manumission. Tiberius' remark makes sense but is not particularly witty.

6. THE EAGLE AND THE CROW

No one is properly protected against the powerful,
And if they are aided by evil advisers,
The effect of force and ferocity combined
Is to overcome all opposition whatever.

An eagle hoisted high in the heavens
A tortoise, which instantly retracted its extremities
And hid in the refuge of its horny home,
Stowed away safely and immune to assaults.
Then a cruising crow came alongside and cried out,
"That's a precious prize you've taken in your talons,
But what will happen when you're weary from the weight?
You'll lose your load, unless you listen to me."
When the eagle had promised him a part of the prize,
The crow counseled him to climb high
And release the reptile over rocky terrain,
Thus cracking the carapace: when this was accomplished,
The flier could easily feast on the flesh.
The eagle accepted this artful advice,
And paid his tutor with a portion of the proceeds.
Thus, the creature that nature had carefully created
Impregnable and invincible in its outward aspect,
Outnumbered now and outmaneuvered,
Died a cruel and dreadful death.

7. THE TWO MULES AND THE ROBBERS

A pair of mules were pursuing their path,
One of them burdened with bags of money,
The other with sacks bulging with barley.
The one with the wealth was prancing proudly,
Which set the bell that swung from his neck
Tinkling tunefully as he tossed his mane,
While his partner plodded placidly behind.
All of a sudden from a secret hideout
There rushed a party of rogues and robbers.
Swords were flashing and slaughter ensued.
In the course of the melee the mule with the money
Was bashed about and robbed of his hoard,
While the other, the bearer of boring barley,
Was beneath their notice and never scratched.
When the wealthy one was bewailing his plight,
The other mused, "I'm mighty glad
To be not worth noticing. Now, as it is,
I have kept my cargo and stayed unscathed."

The moral: that men of modest means
Can disdain the dangers that dog the rich.

8. THE STAG AND THE OXEN

A stag, startled from its sylvan retreat,
In danger of death at the hands of hunters
And frantic with fear, took refuge in a farm
Close by and cowered in a convenient cattle stall.
An ox observed him and asked, amazed,
"What on earth are you after, my unhappy friend,
Of your own accord courting catastrophe
By settling in a stall at the mercy of men?"
The stag pleaded, "Spare me, please:
I'll make a break for it as quickly as I can."
The day declined and dwindled into night.
A cowherd came, carrying branches,
But noticed nothing out of the ordinary.
Farmhands went to and fro, but failed
To spot the stag. The supervisor, even,
Passed down the passageway perfectly oblivious.
The cattle kept quiet, and our captive creature
Began to thank them for giving him sanctuary
In his time of trouble, when one retorted,
"We wish you well, but we want to warn you,
If our many-eyed master makes an appearance,
Without doubt your life will be in deadly danger."
Meanwhile, from his evening meal this master
Returned. He had cause to be concerned for his cattle,
Since they'd looked lately in a sorry state,
So he made for the mangers and found but a meager
Supply of fodder, and no straw to sleep on.
"It wouldn't take them too much trouble,"
He soliloquized, "to clear out these cobwebs."
In the process of probing every particular,
He observed the intruder's enormous antlers.
So he got his staff together and gave them
Orders to slaughter the stag as his spoil.

The moral is that the master is the most
Eagle-eyed observer of his own interests.

9. THE AUTHOR SPEAKS

The Athenians set up a statue to Aesop,
Thereby placing a slave on a permanent pedestal
To the end that all should openly acknowledge
That glory is granted to greatness, not to birth.

Forestalled by another from being first in the field,
I have labored long at the little that was left me,
Namely to ensure that he should not be unique;
And not out of envy, but emulation.
And if my efforts find favor with Rome,
She'll have one more weapon to wield in the challenge
Against Greece; and if green-eyed
Jealousy pleases to disparage my pains,
She will not steal from me my self-esteem.
If my writings are read by people of refinement
Who find that my fables are fashioned skilfully,
My happiness will compensate for all cause for complaint.
But if lesser breeds balk at my book,
Men brought to birth by a boorish Nature,
A kind only capable of criticizing its betters,
I'll endure that exile from the favors of Fortune
With a mind steeled to suffer in silence
Until she blushes for shame and reverses her verdict.

BOOK 3

PROLOGUE: PHAEDRUS TO EUTYCHUS

If you really relish the prospect of reading
My modest volumes, Eutychus, you must take
A break from business and so make your mind
Free to feel their full force.
You protest that my poems are not so precious
As to offset the loss of an hour in the office.
All right: there's really no reason to read
Stuff so unsuitable to your serious concerns.
But perhaps you'll reflect, "I'll have some holidays,
Time free for reading away from work."
Really? Waste time in reading this rubbish
Instead of attending to the things that matter,
Wife, family, friends, refreshment
Of mind and body to make you more
Capable of coping with the requirements of commerce?
If you're minded to enter the mansion of the Muses,
You must change your aspirations and your way of life.
It isn't easy. Why, even I—
Born on the slopes of Pieria* (the place
Where Mnemosyne was nine times made a mother
By Jove, the sire of the sisterhood of singers),†
Practically, I promise, in the precincts of a school,
Who have made myself immune to the lure of money,
And have lived for art, with Athene's aid—
Am grudgingly greeted at the gate of poetry.
A fortiori, what fate will he find
Who spends every second striving to amass
More and more money, whose dreams dwell
On lucre, rather than the labors of learning?

---

* Pieria is a mountainous area on the southeast coast of Macedonia, north of Thessaly.
† The nine Muses.

BOOK 3

53

But "whatever the sequel"* (in the words of Sinon,
When posing as a deserter in Priam's presence),
Here's Volume Three of my versified versions
Of Aesop, dedicated to your distinguished self.
If you read them, good; if they go unread,
At least I will pass the pleasure to posterity.

Now let me give you a little lesson
On why fables, as a form, were first invented.
Slaves are exposed to incessant hazards.
Unable openly to express what he wanted,
One of them projected his personal opinions
Into fictional fables and found shelter
From carping critics in comic inventions.
The lane that he left I've enlarged to a highway
And thought up more themes than he bequeathed,
Though some have got me into terrible trouble.
If my accuser, my judge, and my jury
Had been any other than simply Sejanus,†
I'd have openly acknowledged my evident errors,
And I wouldn't be worrying about saving my name.
I express in advance the hope of being excused.
If people persist in being a prey to suspicion
And mistakenly take themselves to be my targets,‡
When I'm aiming at the obvious errors of all,
The cause is clear: their consciences are guilty.

---

* The quotation is from *Aeneid* 2, 77. Aeneas is describing the fall of Troy to Dido. He tells how the Greek Sinon entered Troy as a spy and persuaded the Trojans to bring the wooden horse into the city. Sinon starts his speech to the Trojans with these words.

† Aelius Sejanus was commander of the Praetorian Guard, consul and confidant of Tiberius, over whom he exercised a pervasive and malign influence. Eventually, Tiberius came to suspect him of planning to supplant him as emperor and denounced him to the senate, which ordered his execution in A.D. 31. No details are known of his prosecution of Phaedrus. It is to be assumed from the fact that Phaedrus speaks of him so freely that this prologue was written after his unlamented death.

‡ Such fables as 1, 1, 1, 2, and perhaps 1, 6, could be taken in this way by people who thought that Phaedrus' intent was subversive.

If I give them pain, I apologize profusely:
My purpose is not to pillory any person,
But to illustrate life and the ways of the world.

"Too taxing a task," a critic may object.
Why so? If the Scythian Anacharsis*
And Aesop the Phrygian found eternal fame
By their innate genius, why should I, who am nearer
To glorious Greece, if you go by the map,
Not hope to be considered a credit to my country?
Our people of Thrace are proud to proclaim
Even gods among the gallery of their great singers—
Apollo, after all, gave life to Linus,†
And a Muse was the mother of the musician Orpheus,‡
Who moved stones by the sweetness of his songs,
Tamed wild creatures, and checked the torrent
Of Hebrus as it lingered limpidly to listen.
So, away with envy, whose efforts will be wasted
When my work is awarded its eternal glory.

Well, Eutychus, have I teased you into reading?
I'd really appreciate your opinion of these poems—
Candid criticism of your customary kind.

---

* Anacharsis was a Scythian sage and philosopher who traveled widely in the Greek world and visited Athens in the time of Solon. Some of his maxims have survived in quotations in Greek authors.
† According to one of several versions, Linus was the son of Apollo and the Argive princess Psamathe.
‡ Orpheus was the son of Apollo and the Muse Calliope.

1. WHAT THE OLD WOMAN SAID TO THE WINE JAR

An old woman once caught sight of a wine jar
Which the drinkers had drunk and left empty.
A fine Falernian this flask had held,
And its dregs still diffused a delicious aroma.
As she eagerly sniffed the scent, she sighed,
"Delightful perfume, how perfect in your prime
You must have been, when your remains are so marvelous."

To people who know me, the point will be plain.*

---

* To us who do not know him, the point is obscure. Since Phaedrus is normally not
averse to spelling out his moral, it seems likely that his intended meaning is somehow subversive and that the wine lees stand for something like the remnant of
freedom.

2. THE PANTHER AND THE SHEPHERDS

Underdogs are apt to avenge themselves
By turning on the people who have plagued or despised them.

When a prowling panther had fallen into a pit,
A group of countrymen gathered to gape,
And some of them pelted her with sticks and stones,
But some felt sorry for the splendid creature,
Destined to die even if not injured,
And flung down some bread to prolong her life.
At nightfall all went away unworried,
Not doubting that they'd find her dead the next day.
Not so. In the night she renewed her strength,
Liberated herself with one leap at daybreak,
And hurried home to her hidden lair.
A brief rest for recuperation,
And down she swooped on the sheep and shepherds
And slaughtered them all in a savage orgy
Of death, destruction, and devastation.
Then even the very villagers who had spared her
Forgot about the loss of their property and only
Pleaded with the panther to preserve their lives.
The panther replied, "You need not be nervous.
I remember who showered me with sticks and stones,
And who fed me with bread. It is only for those
Who chose to hurt me that I harbor hatred."

3. AESOP AND THE FARMER

A person who has learned his lesson from life
Is generally regarded as a safer guide
Than a seer or a soothsayer. The sense of this
I'm the first to explain, with the following fable.

A certain farmer had a flock of sheep
Whose ewes one day gave birth to a brood
With human heads. Horrified by the prodigy,
He rushed off to see what the soothsayers would say.
One of them replied that the aberration
Pointed to peril for the owner, who could only
Avert it by sacrificing a select victim.
Another affirmed that his wife was unfaithful,
That the portent proclaimed spurious children
And could only be expiated by an extraspecial
Immolation of a mature victim.
In short, from each seer a different solution,
Which only aggravated the man's anxiety.
Aesop happened to be standing as a spectator,
That unerring old man whom nothing in nature
Could fool for long, and he counseled as follows:
"My farmer friend, if you want an effective
Cure to counter the recurrence of this conundrum,
I advise you to provide wives for your shepherds."

4. THE BUTCHER AND THE MONKEY

A man saw a monkey among the meat
Hanging from a hook in the butcher's booth,
And asked about its flavor. The fellow said frivolously,
"About as beautiful as the beast itself."

The reply, I presume, was just for a joke,
With no attempt at the truth. For I've often
Known handsome men who had hateful natures,
And ugly types who turned out to be treasures.

5. AESOP AND THE IMPUDENT FELLOW

Success dooms many men to their downfall.

An impudent ass threw a stone at Aesop.
"Good shot!" he shouted, and slipped him a cent,
And added, "I'm afraid it's all I have on me,
But I'll demonstrate how you can make some more.
See that person passing? He's powerful and wealthy.
Sling a stone at him, the same as at me,
And you're bound to get a generous gift."
The idiot was impressed by this bright idea
And did exactly as Aesop had advised.
The outcome, however, was other than expected:
He paid on the cross the penalty for his presumption.

6. THE FLY AND THE MULE

A fly alighted beside a mule
On the wagon pole and rudely rebuked him:
"Come on, get going, for goodness' sake!
What a dawdler! You deserve a deep dig
From my sting, to move you." The mule muttered,
"I couldn't care less about your silly sting.
The fellow sitting on the front seat,
Who steps up my pace with his snaky whip
Or hauls on the bit to hold me back,
That's the fellow who fills me with fear.
So buzz off, boring fly.
Enough of your impudence. I'm well aware
Of the times to loiter and the times to trot."

This fable ridicules, and rightly so,
Men who utter menacing threats
Without the power to put them into effect.

7. THE WOLF AND THE SLEEK DOG

This fable affirms the sweetness of freedom.

A wolf, half-famished and emaciated, met
A well-fed dog, fat and affluent looking.
They exchanged courtesies and came to a stop.
"What a glossy coat," growled the wolf. "My goodness,
What food has put so much flesh on your flanks?
I'm stronger that you, yet I'm simply starving."
The dog gave an honest answer: "It's easy.
Just serve a master, the same way as me."
"By doing what?" "Guard duty at the door,
Night watch to protect the property from plunder.
I don't even beg, and they bring me bread;
My master tosses me tidbits from his table,
And the servants spoil me with surplus delicacies;
Without lifting a finger I feed my fill."
"Sounds splendid," said the wolf; "certainly at present
The life I lead in these lonely woods
Is horribly hard, all hail and snow,
Rain and cold, with no crumb of comfort.
What a boon it would be—a roof over me
And enough food to fill me with no effort."
"Well, join me, then." The wolf jumped for joy,
But just as they were starting he spotted something—
The dog's neck was noose marked or chafed as from a chain.
"What's that mark on your neck?" "Oh, nothing much."
"Come on, what caused it?" "I'm considered restless;
Therefore, in the daytime they tie me with a tether
And keep me quietly confined in a kennel,
So that later, at night, I'm alert and lively.
Then I'm free to wander wherever I wish."
"And let us suppose that you'd like to leave,
Clear out, decamp—can you?" "Well, no."
"So, dog, you keep doing what does you good.
Personally, I prefer to rough it in my freedom.
You wouldn't catch me consenting to be king,
If it made me no longer master of myself."

8. BROTHER AND SISTER

Here's a lesson in self-awareness.

A man had a daughter unusually unattractive,
And a son, by contrast, exceptionally handsome.
One day they were playing in their mother's bedroom
And caught sight of themselves in the looking glass.
The boy began boasting of his beauty; the girl
Lost her temper and resented her brother's bragging.
Interpreting everything as an insult to herself,
She went flying to her father and informed against him
And complained that he'd played with her female parts.
The father caressed them consolingly and kissed them
And lavished his love on both alike.
"I'll give you," he told them, "a daily duty:
Confront yourselves critically in that mirror there;
You, to make sure that you never mar
Your beauty by bad behavior; and you,
To compensate for your plainness by praiseworthy conduct."

9. SOCRATES TO HIS FRIENDS

The word "friendship" is used frequently enough,
But the real thing is rarely found.

When Socrates had selected a site for his house,
A modest place, and had laid the foundations
(I'd happily accept the same fate
As his, if I gained the same fame,
And I'd willingly submit to similar malice
If amends were made to my dust after death),
A character in the crowd commented predictably,
"Such a small shack for such a splendid man?"
"It's small," agreed Socrates, "but, even so,
  How I wish I could fill it with faithful friends."

10. THE POET, ON BELIEVING AND NOT BELIEVING

To believe and not to believe, both are dangerous:
Here's a brief example of each extreme.

Hippolytus met his death because his stepmother
Was believed by Theseus;* and because Cassandra's
Warning was scorned, Troy was destroyed.[†]
So no stone should be left unturned
To find out the truth, before faulty thinking
Leads to a stupid and tragic outcome.
But in case you consider these episodes extravagant,
Being mythical and remote from modern times,
I'll give you an example from my own experience.

A happily married man had a son
About to celebrate his sixteenth birthday.
He was taken aside by his secretary,
An ex-slave, who harbored hopes
Of being substituted for the boy and becoming his heir.
He told some ludicrous lies about the lad,
And more about the immoral conduct
Of the man's wife (a model of chastity),
And he added something that a loving husband
Was bound to find unbearably bitter,
That his wife was receiving regular visits
From a lover, thus loathsomely defiling his house.

---

* Phaedra, wife of Theseus, fell in love with her stepson, Hippolytus. He rejected her
advances, whereupon she hanged herself, having first written a letter to Theseus
denouncing Hippolytus as her seducer. Theseus invoked the vengeance of Poseidon
on Hippolytus and banished him. Poseidon contrived the death of Hippolytus by
sending a monster from the sea, which terrified the horses of his chariot, so that he
was thrown out and dragged to his death.
[†] Because Cassandra, the daughter of Priam and Hecuba, rejected the advances of
Apollo, he made the power of prophecy that he had given her useless, condemning
her not to be believed. Thus, her warnings of the doom of Troy were ignored.

Furious at the fancied falseness of his wife,
The husband pretended to visit his villa
In the country, but in actual fact he lodged
Secretly in the city, and then suddenly at night
Burst into his house and made straight
For his wife's bedchamber, in which by chance
She had made arrangements for her son to sleep,
To guard against dangers to his adolescence.
The scene was chaotic, with servants searching
For lights and milling madly about.
The man, almost insane with rage,
When he got to the bed, groped in the gloom—
A head—short hair—proof enough—
He buried his sword in the sleeper's body,
Heedless of everything except revenge.
When the lights arrived, he saw his son,
And his blameless wife lying nearby
Innocently asleep, and knowing nothing
Of what had happened. The horrified husband
Punished himself for his perverse passion—
Filled with guilt, he fell on the sword
That his stupid credulity had caused him to draw.

Accusers appeared to indict the wife,
And hauled her to Rome to the High Court.
Her innocence was impugned by nasty innuendo,
Since the property had passed to her personal possession.
Fortunately, her friends and supporters stood firm
And doggedly defended the blameless lady.
Then the judges appealed to the Emperor Augustus—
They were conscious of their oath to be absolutely impartial
But were baffled by the complexity of the case.

Augustus cut through the thicket of calumny
And detected the true foundation of the facts.
"Let the person responsible," he pronounced, "be punished:
To wit, the secretary. The woman, without
Both son and husband, I hereby adjudge
A person to be pitied, rather than punished.
If the father of the family had fully investigated
The false charges that were artfully fed to him,
He would not have wreaked havoc on his house and home."

Neither accept nor reject a report
On the spot. The most improbable people,
Outwardly innocent, can be very vicious;
And those far from fault can be fooled and framed.
Let the gullible be guided by this good advice,
And not let others influence their opinions.
The motives of men are many and various:
They can hate and harm you as much as help.
So trust no one you don't know.

I've gone into this question at greater length
Than usual, since a few friends have informed me
That they find my fables somewhat too short.

11. THE EUNUCH'S REPLY TO HIS INSULTING ADVERSARY

A eunuch was engaged in a legal feud
With a nasty type, who, on top of gratuitous
Insults and obscenities, abused the man
For his defective physical faculties.
"True," said the eunuch, "there I'm weaker than you:
I've no testicular evidence of integrity.
But my failing, you fool, is the fault of Fortune:
Why hold it against me? Genuine disgrace
Is to suffer deservedly for deliberate misdeeds."

12. THE COCK AND THE PEARL

A cock was digging desultorily on a dunghill,
Foraging for food, when he found a pearl.
"How splendid," he said, "in such sordid surroundings!
If anyone interested in your intrinsic value
Had come across you, what a coup it would have been—
You'd soon have been restored to your appropriate setting.
Bad luck to be liberated by a lout like me,
Who am far more intent on finding food:
We're neither of us any use to the other."

For people who fail to appreciate my work.

13. THE WASP ADJUDICATING BETWEEN THE BEES AND THE DRONES

The bees had built their honeycombs high up
In the bole of an oak, and the idle drones
Dared to declare that now they were theirs.
The case was consequently brought to court.
The judge, a wasp, who was well aware
Of the characteristics of each class,
Put this proposition to both parties:
"You look quite alike in color and outline,
And a misconception would not be unnatural.
But I have here my duty to do,
And mustn't form opinions from inadequate evidence.
I want you to fill these wax cells
With the products of your respective capacities.
From the savor of the honey and the special shapes
Of the combs it will become quite clear
Who constructed the combs we are now discussing."
The drones demurred, but the bees were pleased
At the test. So the wasp passed sentence as follows:
"It is clear who could and who could not
Have done this work: so I duly declare
That the bees have the benefit of the fruit of their labors."

This object lesson I'd have left unrelated,
Had the drones not refused the stipulated test.*

---

* These last two lines are terse to the point of obscurity. The reference seems to be
to some imitators of Phaedrus who refused a similar challenge to prove their
authenticity.

14. ON PLAY AND SERIOUSNESS

An Athenian citizen once spotted Aesop
Playing marbles* in the middle of some boisterous boys
And laughed aloud—had he taken leave
Of his senses? As soon as Aesop perceived it
(Himself, the master of mockery, being mocked!),
He brought out a bow, unbent and unstrung,
And set it down in the center of the street.
Then he called out, "Come on, my clever friend,
Interpret for us, please, the problem that I've posed you."
A crowd collected. The man racked his brains,
But came no closer to explaining the enigma.
Finally, he confessed his defeat, and Aesop,
The ingenious victor of the exchange, expounded:
"A bow kept bent will break in no time:
But stored unstrung, it will serve you when you need it."

So the mind from time to time should be licensed
To relax at leisure and play a little,
And thus return better to its basic business.

---

* Literally, "nuts," an equivalent game. See Persius, *Satires* 1, 10.

15. THE DOG AND THE LAMB

A dog came across a lost lamb
Floundering about among a flock of goats.
"You're miles from your mother, silly," he said,
"She's there, with those sheep: surely you see them?"
"I'm not looking for her or her kind, who conceive
At their pleasure, carry their compulsory cargo
For a fixed number of months, then finally
Drop the burdensome bundle on the ground.
I'm going to the goat who feeds me from her teat,
And even allows her own offspring
To frisk unfed, rather than fail me."
"But your mother, surely, must mean more
Than a total stranger?" "Not at all.
You think I should thank her for this birthright,
To be bound for nothing but the butcher's block?
Black or white—she could well have borne
Either: no means of knowing. And suppose
She'd hoped to produce a ewe? Disappointment:
All that she managed was me, a male.
Why not prefer the one who pitied me
As I lay there helpless, who now happily
Feeds and fosters me of her own free will
To the one who was bound to bear me blindly?
Kindness, not kinship, constitutes parentage."

The author's aim is to prove that people
React against rules, but succumb to love.

16. THE CICADA AND THE OWL

If you flout the feelings of your fellow men,
You'll probably find yourself punished for your presumption.

A cicada was kicking up a colossal racket,
Which greatly annoyed and upset the owl,
Whose habit was to hunt for sustenance in the darkness
And doze in the daytime in the hollow of a tree.
She asked the cicada to keep quiet,
But the insect only intensified the aggravation.
She tried once more: it got worse and worse.
The owl then, perceiving that the polite appeal
Was getting her nowhere and her words were wasted,
Thought up a stratagem to outwit this chatterbox.
"Since your singing allows me no sleep
(Although it's as lovely as the lyre of Apollo),
I've decided to drink a noggin of nectar,
A present from Pallas. If you'll please join me,
We'll taste it together." Parched by thirst,
And delighted by the lavish compliments on his voice,
The other flew eagerly to accept the invitation.
In brief, the owl blocked the exit behind him,
Caught the terrified creature and consigned him to silence.
So in death he granted what he'd grudged while alive.

17. THE TREES UNDER THE PATRONAGE OF THE GODS

A long time ago the gods were given
The choice of trees to use as their emblems.
Jove chose to be patron of the oak,
Venus and Apollo of the myrtle and laurel,
Cybele and Hercules of the pine and poplar.
Minerva was amazed that they took trees
That produced no fruit. She pursued her enquiries,
Until Jove, as spokesman, explained the cause:
"Our patronage is a pure privilege:
We mustn't be suspected of selling it for the sake
Of reaping the reward of the fruit." "Well, really,
I can't say I care about critical comments.
I like my olive all the better
Precisely because of the bounty of its berries."
The begetter of gods and maker of men
Answered: "My daughter, deservedly are you designated
By all and sundry the wise goddess.
Unless what we do is useful, it is foolish
To boast and brag of our glory and greatness."

Do nothing, says the fable, that is not beneficial.

18. THE PEACOCK COMPLAINS TO JUNO ABOUT HIS VOICE

The peacock plaintively approached Juno,
Feeling sad and slighted that the nightingale
Had been vouchsafed the virtue of a ravishing voice
That amazed all men when they heard her music,
While he, the moment that he opened his mouth,
Was embarrassed by mockery and merriment.
The goddess spoke soothingly to assuage his sorrow:
"But you're fairer by far, more well favored than she,
 With the emerald elegance that enhances your neck
 And the superb spectacle of your outstretched tail,
 The effulgence of feathers in your painted fan."
"A lot of use is this voiceless luster,"
 Replied the peacock, petulant and piqued,
"If my croaking and screeching condemn me to contempt."
"To all animals have been allotted
 Their various virtues by the fiat of Fate.
 You were duly endowed with beauty;
 Eagles are masters of their element of air;
 Sweetness of song belongs supremely
 To nightingales; the raven is graced
 With prophetic power to predict the future;
 To the crow there goes the giving of omens.
 All are satisfied with the status assigned them.
 It's a great mistake to aspire to a nature
 Other than your own: the outcome is only
 Disillusion, despair, and self-deception."

19. AESOP'S REPLY TO THE JOKER

When Aesop was the sole slave of a master,
Being directed one day to cook the dinner
At an unusually early hour, he went round
House after house to find fire,
And reached one at last where he could light his lamp.
On his tour out, the itinerary he had taken
Was rather roundabout: for the route home
He followed a shorter, straight through the forum,
Where a funny fellow yelled, "Hey, Aesop,
Why the lit lamp in broad daylight?"
"I'm looking," he replied, "for a real man."
With which riposte he went on his way.
And if that idiot was interested, he'll have seen
That old Aesop meant that the term "man"
Did not apply to an impertinent pest
Who bothered with his banter a busy person.

EPILOGUE
(To his patron, Eutychus)

There's a mass of material remaining to write about,
But I'm consciously and carefully keeping away from it.
First, I'm afraid you might find it a nuisance,
Distracted as you are by your divers duties;
Second, someone might want to succeed me
In this field of fable, and I felt I should leave
A certain amount of material to mine from;
Though there's such a lot that it's more likely
For the poet to falter than for fables to fail him.

Now I must plead for the prize that you promised me,
The wages of my brevity: be true to your word.
My life draws daily closer to death,
And the longer the time that is allowed to elapse,
The less the profit that I'll perceive from your present.
If you conclude the formalities quickly,
The greater the value I'll get from your gift.
The time when I need assistance is now,
While I still retain some vestiges of vigor.
But once enfeebled by old age,
I'll be beyond the reach of your bounty,
Void then of value, with no power to help me,
And Death will be near to demand his due.
But all this is silly and superfluous,
To sue for your good graces, when I'm well aware
That your compassion comes without being claimed.

It is quite common for an accused person
To be granted pardon for admitting his guilt:
All the more should a guiltless person be pardoned.
You are trying the case; earlier it came up
Before others; and perhaps others in the future
When their turn comes round will be told to try it.
Decide the dispute as your duty dictates,
And I will certainly accept the sentence,
Completely confident in your justice and generosity.

I've gone on too long: but when you're aware
Of your own innocence and absolute integrity,
And find yourself assailed at the same time
By the insults of others eager to injure you,
It's difficult to keep control of your temper.
"Who are these people?" perhaps you wonder.
Just wait. The world will be well aware
In due course. As for me, meanwhile,
So long as my mind retains its reason
I intend to remember a maxim that I read
As a boy: "For a man of humble birth
It is not proper to protest in public."

BOOK 4

PROLOGUE: THE POET TO PARTICULO

After I'd decided to do no more,
In order to ensure enough ore for others
To mine, I privately changed my mind.
For if anyone aspired to rank as my rival,
How could he guess precisely which pieces
I'd intended to deal with in due course?
For those are the ones he'd want to work on
And consign those fables to the keeping of fame,
Making them his own, since men's minds
Are all individual, all different,
And similarly their style. And so I assert
That it's not just caprice that has caused me to commence
Writing once more, but a deliberate decision.
Since, then, Particulo, you're partial to fables
(Which I call Aesopic, not actually Aesop's,
Since I've made more than the few he fathered,
Following his form, but with modern content),
You can now read the following, my fourth volume,
Should you find the time. If malign critics
Want to find fault, I'm quite indifferent—
They can criticize me to their hearts' content,
So long as they can't compete in my craft.
I consider myself adequately recognized
In that you and others in your select circle
Copy my words in your commonplace books:
You clearly consider that they're worth keeping.
In the applause of the unlettered I'm not interested.

1. THE ASS AND THE PRIESTS OF CYBELE

A man marked out for misfortune from birth
Not only lives a luckless life,
But is still dogged after the doom of death
By the same miserable and persistent destiny.

When the Galli (Cybele's priests) used to go
On their begging rounds, they brought with them
An ass, to act as bearer of their baggage.
When he died, worn out with work and whipping,
They flayed him and made from the stretched skin
The tambourines that distinguish their sect.
When someone, horrified, asked them how
They could treat a creature that was practically a pet
In such a way, they phrased it as follows:
"He may have imagined there'd be perfect peace
Beyond the grave, and he may be gone,
But we still give him as good a beating."

2. THE WEASEL AND THE MICE

You say I don't seem to be serious. It's true,
I do have my fun fooling around
When nothing momentous is maturing in my mind,
But even then I'd like you to look
Closely and carefully at these light-weight confections:
They conceal a lot of useful lessons.
They are not always exactly what they seem:
Outward appearances are often deceptive,
And few are favored with a fine enough sense
To discover what the artist has concealed in a corner.
To avoid being accused of speaking in the abstract,
I'll prove my point by appending an example,
A moral fable about the weasel and the mice.

A weasel, weary and weak from old age,
Unable to overtake the agile mice,
Rolled in some flour and flung herself
Casually down in a dark corner.
A mouse, assuming it was something to eat,
Pounced on it, was entrapped, and was put to death.
A second and third similarly succumbed,
And so on. In the end there arrived on the scene
A gnarled and knowing old campaigner,
Who'd escaped from many a snare and mousetrap.
He divined from a distance the dirty trick
Of this cunning creature and cried out, "Good luck!
My wish, I assure you, is just as sincere
As is your façade of being honest flour."

3. THE FOX AND THE GRAPES

A famished fox was frantically jumping
To get at some grapes that grew thickly,
Heavy and ripe on a high vine.
In the end he grew weary and gave up, thwarted,
And muttered morosely as he moved away:
"They're not worth reaching—still raw and unripe;
I simply can't stomach sour grapes."

Those who belittle what's beyond their ability
Should see if this story applies to themselves.

4. THE HORSE AND THE WILD BOAR

A wild boar, wallowing weightily around,
One day muddied and made murky
A stretch of shallow and secluded water
Where a horse was in the habit of having his drink.
So a quarrel started between the two.
Clatter-hooves, convulsed with rage at the creature,
Approached a man and asked for an alliance.
He allowed the man to mount on his back,
And carried him confidently to confront their antagonist.
The horseman with his spears made short work
Of the boar beneath him, then addressed his ally:
"How glad I am that I agreed to help you!
I've bagged this big game, and I've gained the knowledge
Of how useful you are." And he harnessed him up,
In spite of his protests, with bit and bridle.
Then the horse morosely muttered, "How misguided,
What a fool I feel! I was full of resentment
And vowing vengeance for a negligible nuisance,
And here I end up exploited forever."

This story should serve as a salutary warning
To the angry and aggressive that it's always better
To bear with being hurt without hitting back
Than be put in the power of another person.

5. AESOP AND THE ENIGMATIC WILL

One man can be worth more than a multitude:
This short story will show you how.
A man at his death left three daughters.
One was a beauty, who beguiled and bewitched
With alluring looks; the second loved
Spinning and a simple rustic existence;
The third was ugly and indulged unduly
In drink. Now the man had made their mother
His heir, on the curious condition that she carve up
The complete sum equally among the three,
But on these terms: "they must not own
Or enjoy the use of the gifts they are given";
And a second condition, "as soon as they have ceased
To hold the property that has passed into their possession,
They must make over to their mother the amount
Of twenty-five thousand pounds apiece."
Athens was abuzz with the news. The mother
Went bustling about consulting lawyers,
But none succeeded in solving the problem
Of how the heirs could avoid owning
Or enjoying the use of the gifts they were given;
Nor, again, how heirs who had nothing to their name
Could manage to pay money to their mother.
All this took a long time, and still
The meaning of the will remained a mystery.
So the lady, ignoring the letter of the law,
Had recourse to equity and common sense.
To the fashionable daughter went the fine dresses,
The brooches, the bracelets, and the beautiful pearls,
The silver ewers and the smooth eunuchs;
To the rustic sister, the spinner of wool,
A flourishing farm, with flocks and cattle,
A house, farm hands, acres, and equipment;
To the drinker, a cellar complete with casks
Of vintage wine, an elegant villa,
Finely furnished, and a charming garden.

She was just going to give to each of the girls
Their appointed property, with approval from the public,
Who knew their natures, when out of the crowd
Emerged Aesop, and exclaimed, outraged,
"If their late father could come back to life,
How angry he'd be that the Athenians were unable
To interpret the strict terms of his testament!"
He then explained where they'd made their mistakes:
"Give the villa, with its furniture and fine cellar
And its elegant gardens, to the country bumpkin.
The fashionable clothes, the frills, and the footmen,
Those should go to the daughter who drinks.
The farmhouse, the fields, the flocks, and the rustics
Should be given to the girl who lives for glamour.
None will put up with the appalling prospect
Of keeping legacies so absolutely alien
To all their interests. The ugly daughter
Will sell off the wardrobe to buy her wine.
The worldly woman will let go her lands
To acquire her beautiful clothes. The bumpkin
Will hand over her handsome house
At any price, to get back to her cattle
And the wool and weaving she misses so much.
The result will be that none of these people
Will have the ownership of the gifts they were given,
And out of the price paid for their possessions
They'll bestow the stated sum on their mother."

So the problem that baffled the brains of the public
Was solved by the subtlety of a single person.

6. THE BATTLE OF THE MICE AND WEASELS

Beaten in battle by a band of weasels
(Plenty of our taverns have pictures portraying it),
The mice in a rout were milling madly
Round the entrances to their holes in their eagerness to escape.
A hard time they had of it reaching their refuge,
But they did squeeze in and escape destruction—
All, that is, except the army's officers,
Who had fastened horns on their heads to help them
Be clearly recognized by the ranks as commanders.
These got stuck in the entrances and taken captive,
And they glutted as victims the voracious victor,
Who gulped them down into his greedy guts.

When catastrophe comes to overwhelm a country,
It's the powerful people who are exposed to danger:
Plain folk are protected by their unimportance.

7. PHAEDRUS AND THE CRITIC

Supercilious critic, who turn up your nose
At the things I write and think it beneath you
To read my ribald and trivial productions,
Persevere patiently, please, with this book,
While I try to accommodate you by introducing Aesop
In a novel guise, in the garb of tragedy:
    I wish the pine had never fallen beneath
    The ax's blow on Pelion's forest height;
    I wish that Argus never had constructed
    With Pallas' help the fatal ship that sailed
    On that doomed, valiant voyage and first explored
    The Euxine's inhospitable domains—
    The bane of Greeks and foreigners alike.
    For now Aeëtes' proud house lies in mourning,
    And Pelias' realm is stricken by the crime
    Of fell Medea, subtle sorceress,
    Who, in her flight from Colchis, slowed pursuit
    By strewing on the sea her brother's limbs,
    That brother whom she'd killed, and here in Greece
    Suborned the daughters of King Pelias
    To stain their hands red with their father's blood.

How do you find it? "Also flat and feeble;
Besides, a lie. For long before that
Minos had made himself master of the Aegean
With the first fleet, and formed the model
Of a great empire governed by law."
You're more critical than crotchety Cato.
There's no pleasing you: you protest against
Frivolous fables, and now tragedy, too.
You'd better leave literature entirely alone,
Or you may find it bites back at you.

I've aimed this attack at those asinine people
Who express their disgust at almost everything,
And, to get themselves credit for being sharp critics,
Are even ready to rail against heaven.

8. THE VIPER AND THE FILE

Anyone who bares his teeth and bites
A person who turns out to bite harder
Will see himself in the story that follows:

A viper invaded a blacksmith's shop
In search of food and fastened its fangs
On an iron file, which disdainfully addressed it:
"D'you imagine you can make an impression on me,
Who can eat through any iron in existence?"

9. THE FOX AND THE GOAT

When a crafty character comes into danger,
He engineers his escape at another's expense.

A fox had fallen fortuitously in a well
And was held there helpless under the high rim,
When along came liberation in the guise of a goat
To the same place, hoping to slake his thirst.
He asked the fox, "Is it fresh and plentiful,
The water down there?" Our wily fox
Dreamed up a sudden and deceitful scheme:
"Come on down, my friend: this draft is so delicious,
I could go on enjoying it forever and ever."
Bearded billy went blundering down,
Thus enabling the ingenious fox to escape.
For he hoisted himself on those huge horns
And leapt out lightly from the well, leaving
Poor goat engulfed in his watery gaol.

10. ON THE FAULTS OF MEN

Two bags full of faults have been fitted onto us
By Jupiter, one weighed down by our own,
Hanging behind us, the other heavy
With other people's, plainly pendant
In front of us, easy for our eyes to observe.

Which is why we are blind to our own vices,
But sharp critics of the shortcomings of others.

11. THE THIEF AND HIS LAMP

A thief lit his lamp from the flame that burned
On Jupiter's altar, and then robbed the god
Of the priceless treasures stored in the temple,
Using for the purpose the purloined light,
Jove's own. He was leaving, laden with loot,
The proceeds of his sacrilege, when all of a sudden
Holiness personified hailed him and spoke:
"The gold you have stolen was gifts from the wicked,
And therefore repugnant to true Religion,
And the theft is nothing; nevertheless,
Your intention was evil, and you'll pay the penalty
In due course, when the day of destiny
Comes and punishes you with the loss of your life.
But I mean to ensure that our fire, in future,
Which lights the pious in their prayers and praise,
Will not be allowed to illuminate crime.
From henceforth, no more transmission of my flame."
Thus, to this day the sacred fire
May never be used to light a lamp,
Nor a lamp used to light a sacrifice.

There are useful lessons to be learned for life
From this moral fable, and no one has the knowledge
Except the author to explain their import.
First, it demonstrates that the direst danger
Can come from those you've carefully cherished;
Second, that criminals are not castigated
By the vengeful anger of outraged gods,
But in due time by decree of destiny;
And last, to the good it gives grave warning
Against sharing the use of anything with the evil.

12. THE EVILS OF WEALTH

Riches are hated by heroes—and rightly:
They deflect praise from its proper objects.

When Hercules was received into the heights of heaven,
The reward for his acts of valor and virtue,
And the gods had greeted him with congratulations,
He replied with pleasure; but when Plutus appeared
(The child of the fickle goddess Fortune)
He averted his eyes in silence. When asked
By his father, Jupiter, for the reason for his rudeness,
He answered, "How can I help hating him?
He's the friend and favorite of all who are evil,
And the archcorrupter who lures with lucre."

13. THE REIGN OF THE LION

"Nothing benefits more than to tell the truth."
Of course, we should all commend this moral:
But sincerity sometimes has disastrous results.

When the lion had made himself lord of the animals
And desired a reputation for straight dealing,
He entirely abandoned his habitual behavior
And with unfailing fidelity honorably upheld
The letter of the law. But it didn't last.
His resolve to be reformed slowly slipped,

Note: There are three problems in connection with this fable:
   (a) It is incomplete. Fortunately we have a medieval prose paraphrase that
       completes it.
   (b) The moral at the beginning is not appropriate to the fable, which in the
       medieval prose version has a different one.
   (c) This leaves the moral unanchored to a fable. One editor has added it to
       another fable, "The King of the Apes," which it suits well. This fable is
       not in Phaedrus, but a prose version is found in the same collection that
       has "The Reign of the Lion."
   For both prose versions, see L. Hervieux, *Les Fabulistes Latins* (Paris: 1893–1894;
   reprinted New York: Burt Franklin, undated), vol. 2, pp. 223 and 227.
Herewith verse translations of both fables as reconstituted according to the above
   notes and numbered 13A and 13B.

13A. THE REIGN OF THE LION

There are times when the penalties for speaking out
And for keeping quiet are equally awful.

When the lion had made himself lord of the animals
And desired a reputation for straight dealing,
He entirely abandoned his habitual behavior
And with unfailing fidelity honorably upheld
The letter of the law. But it didn't last.
His resolve to be reformed slowly slipped,
And he found himself unable to change his nature.
He started taking his subjects aside
And trapping them all with a tricky question:
"Does my breath smell?" And both the beasts
Who answered in the affirmative and those who said "No"
Were similarly slaughtered to sate his appetite
For blood. By and by he came to the ape
And asked him also about his breath.
The ape answered, "Beautiful. Beatific.
Something like cinnamon, or the subtle spices
That smell so glorious on the altars of the gods."
The lion blushed to behave so badly
To one who had praised him in such poetic phrases;
But, determined to deceive him all the same,
He changed his tactics with a new trick
And pretended instead to be suffering from a sickness.
Doctors were summoned, and examined his veins:
His pulse was steady. They prescribed a diet,
Light and digestible—as luxurious as he liked,
For kings can command any kind they fancy.
"I'd like to try something I've never tasted,"
He musingly said, "the meat of a monkey."
No sooner said than done. The simian,
For all his fawning and flattery, was slaughtered
For the lion to be fed forthwith on his flesh.

13B. THE KING OF THE APES

"Nothing benefits more than to tell the truth."
Of course, we should all commend this moral:
But sincerity sometimes has disastrous results.

Two men, one truthful and the other a trickster,
Were traveling together. In the course of time
They came into a country controlled by the apes.
When the apes had watched them for a while, the one
Who appeared to stand in authority ordered
The travelers to be detained, in order to question them
And discover what humans were saying about himself.
He ordered the other apes to be paraded
In a long line to his left and right,
And a throne to be set facing them for himself
(He'd seen the Emperor do the same at a ceremony).
The men were marched in and stood in the middle
And he asked the liar, "Who am I?"
The answer came quickly, "The Emperor, of course."
"And these whom you see standing at my feet?"
"Your courtiers, councilors, chamberlains and captains."
This flattery fooled them all, and his falsehoods
Were duly rewarded. Then the truthful traveler
Said to himself, "If this sly liar
Gets a big reward, I'm bound to be given
An even bigger if I tell the truth."
The apes' leader repeated his query:
"Who am I, and who are these you see at my feet?"
"You're an ape, as always, and all these assembled
Are apes also, and always will be."
Attacked instantly with tooth and claw,
He was torn to pieces for telling the truth.

14. PROMETHEUS

(A fragment)*

Then, having produced her private parts,
From the same material he immediately made
The woman's tongue—and to that we can trace
The true source of their similar obscenity.

---

* In Greek mythology there are conflicting accounts of the creation of man. Phaedrus follows the version that gives the credit to the Titan Prometheus, the great potter-craftsman who made man out of clay and water. See also Fables 4, 15 and Perotti 5-6.

15. PROMETHEUS AGAIN

Then somebody asked old Aesop
What paradoxical process had produced
Men-women and vice versa.
"This same Prometheus," he explained, "who made
Our folk, fashioned from such fragile clay
That it shatters as soon as it's assaulted by Fortune—
This Prometheus had spent the day producing
In separated piles those two parts
Which decency demands to be concealed by clothes,
Intending to attach them later to their respective
Bodies. But Bacchus unexpectedly
Invited him to dinner. He indulged deeply
In heavenly nectar and only got home
Late at night, with unsteady steps.
Then with heavy head and drunken fumbling
He fitted female fixtures onto males,
And members meant for males onto females.
And that's why today we all too often
See passion diverted into depraved paths."

16. THE BEARDED SHE-GOATS

When the female goats had been graciously granted
The favor of wearing beards by Jove,
The males were incensed and expressed their indignation
That the women had won equality with themselves.
"Let them revel," he replied, "in their empty splendor
And adopt the adornment that was distinctive to you,
So long as they can't compete with you in courage."

This story teaches you to tolerate it when those
Who are not comparable in character or capacity
Assume the same uniform as you.

17. ON THE FORTUNES OF MEN

When a man was moaning about the meanness of Fortune,
Aesop invented this allegory to console him.

A boat had been badly battered by a storm,
And the passengers were in a panic at the prospect of death,
When the danger suddenly died down,
The skies cleared, the sun shone,
And she bowled along under a brisk breeze.
This raised the spirits of the sailors excessively;
But, made wise in the ways of the wind and water
By long experience, the pilot reproved them:
"All life is laced with sorrow and gladness.
So be careful of rejoicing or complaining too quickly."

18. THE DOGS SEND ENVOYS TO JUPITER

The dogs sent a delegation to Jupiter
To plead for a lighter lot in their lives
And deliverance from the drudgery and degradation
Meted out by men, who made a mixture
Of bread and bran to abate their appetite,
And other much worse, unmentionable matter.
Off went the ambassadors, but far from fast—
So busy sniffing for scraps in dung heaps
That when hailed by name they failed to answer.
Finally, Mercury managed to maneuver them
Into the building, blushing and embarrassed;
But then, when confronted face to face
With solemn Jupiter, they were so scared
That all over his mansion they made their messes.
They were turned out promptly from the precincts of the palace
By kicks and cudgels, but the King of the Gods
For some reason made them stay in the vicinity.
Meanwhile, the dogs who had dispatched the deputation
Were anxious at the long absence of their ambassadors.
Suspecting that something discreditable had been done
By those envoys, they ordered others to be appointed.
Then rumor betrayed the unsavory behavior
Of the first envoys, and fearing there might follow
A similar disaster from the second set,
They stuffed their behinds with beatific perfumes
And gave them their instructions. They started off,
Requested an audience, and were admitted at once.
The mighty maker of men and gods
Sat there enthroned, and threatened with his thunderbolts;
Everything shook; the shattering crash
Dismayed the dogs, who did their business
Instantly—a mixture of myrrh and muck.

The immortals immediately insisted that this insult
Must be avenged. But before justice
Was duly dispensed, Jupiter dictated:
"It is not the royal prerogative to prevent
The departure of delegates; nor is it difficult
To impose a proper punishment for their offense.
So I let them depart; but in addition I decree
That the creatures be constantly wracked by hunger,
To help them hold the contents of their stomachs.
As for those who sent such despicable specimens
Twice in a row to represent their race,
I pronounce them objects of perpetual opprobrium
In the eyes of men."
                              And as to the envoys—
Their descendent dogs to this day are awaiting
Their return. Which is why, whenever a strange dog
Appears on the scene, they start sniffing his posterior.

19. THE SNAKE FATAL TO THE COMPASSIONATE MAN

(Textual version)

A man saw a snake stiff from the cold
And picked it up and put it, out of pity,
Against his body to restore its warmth.
He was kind and compassionate to his own cost,
For the snake was no sooner resuscitated
Than it killed the man. When questioned by a comrade
As to why it had done such a dreadful deed,
It replied, "To offer an object lesson
Against misplaced mercy to malicious creatures."

19A. THE SNAKE FATAL TO THE COMPASSIONATE MAN
(With the ending as emended by Pieter Burman)

A man saw a snake stiff from the cold
And picked it up and put it, out of pity,
Against his body to restore its warmth.
He was kind and compassionate to his own cost,
For the snake was no sooner resuscitated
Than it stung him to death.
                              When pressed to explain
Why I had depicted such a dreadful deed,
I answered, "To offer an object lesson
Against misplaced mercy to malicious creatures."

20. THE FOX AND THE DRAGON

A fox was hollowing a hole for his house.
As he dug deeper and deeper into the ground,
He suddenly came upon the concealed cave
Of a dragon, who was guarding a hidden hoard.
As soon as he saw him, he started to speak:
"Please excuse this unintentional intrusion;
And since you must see how unsuited to my style
Is all this gold, I'd be glad if you'd give me
An answer to my enquiry: what actual profit
Do you derive from this drudgery? And does it
Compensate you for keeping constantly awake
And dragging out your life in this dreary darkness?"
"No profit," he replied, "but that's not the point.
I was simply given this assignment by supreme
Jupiter." "You enjoy, then, no personal profit,
And don't pass on anything to anyone else?"
"So Destiny has decided." "Please don't be angry
If I speak plainly: a person like you
Must have been begotten with the gods against him."

You're bound for the same bourn as others before you,
So why make miserable this mortal life
And blindly embitter it with self-torment?
It's you I mean, morose miser,
You who give hope of happiness to your heir,
Who begrudge the gods the gift of incense
And starve yourself of your own supper,
Who listen listlessly to the lyre and the flute,
Who groan with pain at the price of provisions,
Who increase your capital cent by cent
And repel the gods by perjuries in the process,
And are constantly cutting down the cost of your funeral,
So that, when the time comes, the undertakers
Can't possibly profit at the expense of your estate.

21. PHAEDRUS

What meanness is maturing in the mind of Malice?
He may try to hide it, but I'm well aware
Of what it will be. All the parts of my work
That are worth preserving and passing to posterity
He will say are Aesop's; all the less satisfactory
Sections he will swear have been composed by me.
I hereby offer my definitive refutation:
Whatever is weak or worthwhile in this work,
The source is the same. Aesop conceived it,
And I fashioned it in felicitous form.
And now, with your consent, I'll continue on my course.

22. ABOUT SIMONIDES

A man with a mind, wherever he moves,
Constantly carries his wealth with him.

Simonides, singer of such famous songs,
Hoping to improve his impoverished condition,
Went off on a visit to the brilliant cities
Of Asia Minor, to make money
From odes in honor of victorious athletes.
By this lucrative practice he prospered greatly,
And so decided to sail home
(He came, of course, from the island of Ceos).
He boarded a ship, which had no sooner sailed
Than a sudden storm struck its aging timbers
Full amidships and made it founder.
Panic. People were packing their treasures,
Things that would serve to support their existence,
Gold or jewels, in belts and bags.
One more inquisitive than the others inquired,
"Simonides, do you need nothing?"
"All that I have is here with me,"
He replied. Most of the people perished,
Dragged down and drowned by the weight of their wealth,
But some succeeded in swimming ashore.
They had hardly got there, when a gang of bandits
Swooped down and stripped them of their prized possessions,
Leaving them with nothing. Now, there lay nearby
The historic city of Clazomenae,
And to this the survivors struggled. As it happened
There lived there a learned and literary person
Who had read and re-read and admired from afar
Simonides' verses. From his very speech
He immediately recognized Simonides, the master,
And invited him home, where he heaped him with honors,
Clothed and looked after him, and loaded him with gold.

An opposite fate had overtaken the others,
Victims of the wreck—reduced to going round
Begging for bread and bearing before them
Placards that depicted their perils by shipwreck.
Simonides, happening to meet them, remarked,
"I told you at the time I was taking with me
All that I had. You, who panicked to preserve
Your precious possessions, have lost them all."

23. THE MOUNTAIN IN LABOR

A mountain was in labor and moaning monstrously,
And the earth was expecting an amazing outcome;
But all that it bore was a minuscule mouse.

Which fable is fashioned as a metaphor for men
Whose claims are colossal, their accomplishments nil.

24. THE ANT AND THE FLY

An ant and a fly were furiously disputing
As to which one of them was the more important.
The fly spoke first: "I fail to understand you.
How can you compare your qualities with mine?
I idle all day among the altars,
I traverse the temples, and taste before anyone
The burnt offerings at solemn sacrifices;
I can perch when I please on the King's pate,
Or savor the kisses of chaste ladies;
I laze around in the lap of luxury.
Can you claim to compete, my country cousin?"
"To dine with the gods is definitely a distinction—
But only if you are honorably invited,
Not if you're nothing but a nuisance and intruder.
As for your persistent presence at altars:
You've no sooner settled than you're swished away.
You talk about your contact with kings, and the kisses
Of fine ladies and further delights
That decency should induce you to keep secret.
You idle and loiter lazily along,
So in time of need you've nothing to your name.
While I'm getting grain together for the winter,
You're flitting about and feeding on filth;
But when December wizens you and you die,
I'm decently sheltered in my well-stocked dwelling.
You insult me in the summer: when the cold comes, you're
    quiet.
That's plenty, I fancy, to put down your pride."

This story distinguishes two types:
The sheer show-offs with nothing to support
Their airy pretensions and, contrariwise,
The solid citizens who deserve their status.

25. SIMONIDES SAVED BY THE GODS

I have shown how highly poetry is prized
Among mortal men. I mean to show now
How greatly it is also honored by the gods.

That same Simonides of whom I have spoken
Was commissioned by a boxer for a stipulated sum
To compose an ode in honor of his Olympic
Success. He settled down in seclusion to work.
When the thinness of the theme inhibited his invention,
He had recourse, as is commonly the case,
To the poet's freedom, and put into the piece
The twin stars, Castor and Pollux,
As models and masters of the manly art.
The work was welcomed, but the reward was only
A third of the total promised in the contract.
He requested the rest. The reply came:
"That pair whose praises occupy two-thirds
Of your poem can pay you the portion you are missing.
But to show that there's no ill feeling from me,
I invite you to dine tonight at my house.
Some kinsmen of mine are coming, and I count you
As one of them." Simonides, though smarting
From the treatment, and feeling cheated, agreed,
Being reluctant to ruin his reputation
With his patrons by parting on petulant terms.
At the stated time he took his seat
At the banqueting table, which was bright and festive—
Wine flowed freely, and the whole house
Glittered luxuriously and was lively with laughter.
Then two young men, dusty from travel
And soaked in sweat, suddenly appeared
At the door, taller in stature than mortals.

They ordered a servant to send for Simonides.
He must come immediately: the matter was urgent.
The man was puzzled, but apprised the poet.
Simonides followed him, and had hardly set
One foot beyond the banqueting hall,
When its roof caved in and crushed the company,
Killing them all. And, curiously, at the gate
There was not a vestige of the strange visitors.

When these events, as narrated, were known,
Everyone understood that the intervention
Of the gods in person had given the poet
His life, in lieu of the lost payment.

EPILOGUE: THE POET TO PARTICULO

There are plenty of topics left that I could treat—
The amount and variety available are abundant—
But pleasantries which, when controlled, are welcome,
When carried beyond due bounds are boring.
Therefore, Particulo, whom I honor so highly,
Whom these pages of mine will make remembered
As long as Latin literature is valued,
I expect your good estimate, if not of my talent,
At least of my brevity; which has all the better
Claim on your consideration as the common run
Of poets are wearisome and long-windedly magniloquent.

BOOK 5

PROLOGUE: THE POET AGAIN

I've already acknowledged what I owed Aesop.
And if anywhere I insert his name again,
I'm doing it purely to profit from his prestige.
That's the way things are: there are artists today
Who get much more money for their modern works
If they sign their statues "Praxiteles,"
Their silverware "Mys," or their paintings "Zeuxis."
The public, in fact, prefers spurious
Antiques to the products of the present day,
However good—out of jealousy and envy.
I offer a fable that is roughly relevant.*

---

* The fable that follows is not at all relevant. It has been suggested that such a fable
was contained in a continuation, now lost, of this prologue.

1. KING DEMETRIUS AND THE POET MENANDER

King Demetrius, who was called Phalereus,*
Occupied Athens by an unlawful act.
The crowd swarmed round, competing as usual
In abject flattery and felicitations. The foremost
Citizens kissed the hand that oppressed them,
While inwardly groaning at the grim shifts
Of fickle fortune. Finally, even
The people who lived lives of leisure
Quietly in the country came crawling in,
Anxious to avoid offending by their absence.
Among them was Menander, the master of comedy,
Whom Demetrius had read, admiring his genius
Without ever meeting the man in person.
Well, he duly came, drenched in cosmetics,
In flowing robes, and floating along
With a languid, licentious, and lascivious walk.
When the tyrant spotted him, last in the line,
He asked indignantly, "Who on earth
Is that effeminate freak with the effrontery
To posture like a cheap prostitute in my presence?"
"Why, that's Menander, the renowned writer."
At once he went back on his words, and observed,
"A handsomer fellow you'd go far to find."

---

* Phaedrus seems to have confused the Athenian Demetrius of Phalerum with his
contemporary Demetrius Poliorcetes of Macedon, who occupied Athens in 307 B.C.
The story makes no sense with Demetrius of Phalerum, since he was a friend of
Menander and had been educated with him in the school of Theophrastus.

2. THE TWO SOLDIERS AND THE ROBBER

Two soldiers traveling together
Were waylaid by a robber. One of them vanished,
The other stood firm and fought fiercely.
When he'd routed the robber, his cowardly companion
Came bustling back, full of bluster and bravado,
Cast off his cloak, unsheathed his sword,
And cried, "Let him come! He'll learn quickly enough
Whom he has attacked!" Then the man who had grappled
Bravely with the robber and beaten him off
Replied, "I wish you'd been with me—those words,
If nothing else, I needed just now:
I'd have fought better just believing you meant it.
You can sheathe your sword and spare me your speeches:
I find both equally false and futile.
You may be able to bamboozle others
Who know nothing about you, but not me.
I've been warned and made only too well aware
With what speed you can take to your heels,
And how completely your courage can be discounted."

This applies to people who are paragons of bravery
When the situation's safe, but run when it's risky.

3. THE BALD MAN AND THE FLY

A bald man was bitten on his bared head
By a fly. In trying to consign it to its death
He hit himself so hard that it hurt him badly.
The fly made fun of him: "You fancied you'd avenge
The sting of a little insect with death.
What penalty do you propose for your own person
For adding to the injury you intended for me
The stupid insult of a slap to yourself?"
The man retorted, "It'll be no trouble
To get myself back into my good graces,
Since I'm well aware that I wasn't intending
To maim myself. But you, miserable member
Of a disgusting species, who take pleasure in sipping
The blood of humans—to have you removed,
I'd gladly pay a more painful penalty."

This example shows that to err by accident
Is pardonable. But to do damage deliberately
Deserves any punishment, in my opinion.

4. THE ASS AND THE PIG'S BARLEY

A certain person had sacrificed a pig
To the hero Hercules, to whom he owed
Fulfillment of a prayer for the preservation of his life.
He arranged for the residue of the pig's barley
To be served to the ass, who refused it, saying:
"I'd be quite keen to accept that food,
If the one for whom it was originally intended
Had not been chosen to have his throat cut."

The warning of this fable has made me wary
Of pursuing profit that involved peril.
"Plenty of people," you reply, "who pilfer
Go on enjoying their ill-gotten gains."
Come then, let's count the number who are caught
And pay for it: you'll find they are far more.
Reckless adventurism brings a big bonus
To a few men, but misfortune to most.

5. THE BUFFOON AND THE COUNTRYMAN

It often happens that people, through prejudice,
Make mistakes and, maintaining stubbornly
Their false positions, are forced by the facts
To recant in the end and admit their errors.

A rich man was planning to give a grand
Entertainment and invited anyone interested,
With the promise of a prize, to perform in public,
Introducing an original act.
All the artistes entered the contest.
Among them was one well known
For ingenious bits of business, a buffoon,
Who announced an act unparalleled in the theatre.
The rumor stirred up much excitement in the city;
Places usually vacant were taken,
And the auditorium couldn't contain the crowd.
As soon as he stood on the stage, alone,
Without any apparatus or assistants,
The crowd subsided into dead silence.
Suddenly, he drew in his chin to his chest,
And with exact intonations mimicked a pig
With such skill that the crowd, convinced
That he'd concealed a real one under cover of his cloak,
Shouted to him to shake out the folds.
He did so, and thus demonstrated that he'd done it himself,
Whereupon they praised him and applauded passionately.
A visitor was there from a village, who vowed,
"I bet I can beat him," and then boasted
That he'd outdo the act the next day.
The crowd, curious, came in for the contest.

Prejudiced, they had previously picked their favorite
And were there to jeer, not to judge justly.
The two contestants came on the stage,
And the successful joker started, and squealed,
And grunted again through the gamut of his sounds.
Cheers and clapping. Then the clown from the country
Pretended he'd put a pig under his clothes
(Which in fact he had, though having been fooled
By the first buffoon, they refused to believe it).
Then he pinched the ear of the pig he had hidden,
And forced from it a fearful shriek.
The crowd cried out that the clown yesterday
Had represented the pig's pain much better,
And started to boo him from the stage. But he stood there
And produced the pig from the place where he'd hidden it
In the folds of his cloak, and disclosed to the crowd
By patent evidence the proof of their stupid
And shameful mistake. "That'll show you," he shouted,
"Just what kind of judges you gentlemen are!"

6. THE TWO BALD MEN

A bald man came by chance on a comb
Lying in the street. A stranger, similarly
Hairless, who happened to be passing, cried, "Hey!
Fair shares of fortunate finds!"
The other displayed what he had, and added,
"The gracious gods have given us a prize;
But fate has been against us, and we've found, I'm afraid,
Coal instead of gold, as the proverb goes."

People disappointed by hope will perceive
That this complaint is applicable to their case.

7. KING, THE FLUTE PLAYER

When a frivolous mind is made complacent
By the wayward winds of popular applause
And assumes an attitude of arrogant assurance,
Its pretensions are easily pricked by ridicule.

King, the flautist, was accustomed to accompanying
The dancer Bathyllus* in his stage shows
And consequently became something of a celebrity.
At some games or other (I've forgotten which ones)
When the stage machinery was being manipulated, he managed
To fall and fracture his left shin bone—
He'd have borne better the breakage of his instruments.†
In great pain, he was picked up by his supporters
And carried home. The healing process
Was long and slow. And, since spectators
Are a good-natured and generous group,
He was sadly missed as the man whose music
Did so much to enhance the dancing.
A distinguished patron was on the point of producing
A special show, and it so happened
That King was sufficiently cured to use crutches.
The patron appealed to him with pleas and presents
To put in an appearance on the day of the performance.
On the day, rumors about the flute player
Swept through the theatre: some said he was dead,
Others that he was supposed to make an appearance.
The curtain went up—a rumble of thunder,
And the gods began talking in their traditional style.

---

* Bathyllus' name sets this anecdote in the period of Augustus, since he was a favorite
of Maecenas.
† There is a play on words here that I have failed to reproduce, based on the fact that
tibia means both a shin bone and a flute.

Then the chorus started singing a song
(Unfamiliar to our friend, who'd been far from the theatre)
Whose refrain ran, "Rejoice, Rome,
Your state is safe, now the King has recovered."
Applause. Our friend, leaping to his feet,
Began blowing kisses, believing the ovation
Was intended for himself. In their special seats
In the front rows, the important people
Caught on quickly to King's misunderstanding,
And with roars of laughter ordered an encore.
Once more the same song was sung.
Our hero hurried to the stage and happily
Bowed to the crowd. Applause, and howls
Of mocking laughter from the men in front,
And the public presumed that they proposed to bestow
The usual reward of a wreath on the flautist.*
When the truth dawned on the tiers of spectators,
King, elegant, with his lame leg
In a white bandage, and wearing a white
Shirt and shoes, still shamelessly assuming
That the honors intended for the emperor were his,
Was ejected from the theatre by general consent.

---

* The translation follows Shackleton-Bailey's emendation: *rogari populus huic coronam aestimat.*

BOOK 5

8. TIME

He's as fleet of foot as a flying bird,
Perfectly poised on a precise edge,
Completely bald at the back of his head *
But wearing a flourishing forelock on his forehead—
If you grasp him from the front, you can get a grip,
But once he's permitted to slip past,
Not Jupiter in person can bring him back:
His image expresses the elusiveness of opportunity.

The ancients invented this emblem of Time
To stop us from spoiling our projects through sloth.

---

* The text of the first two lines of the Latin is very uncertain. I read, with Postgate,
nudo occipitio, "with the back of his head bald." This fable is based on a famous statue
by Lysippus, contemporary with Alexander the Great.

9. THE BULL AND THE CALF

A bull was badly hampered by his horns
While trying to return through a narrow passage
To his stall in the stables, and kept getting stuck.
When a callow calf tried to come to his rescue
With useful tips about twisting and turning,
The bull bellowed, "Before you were born
I'd learnt from experience your superfluous suggestions."

So don't presume to give impertinent precepts
To those wiser than you in the ways of the world.

10. THE OLD DOG AND THE HUNTER

A dog who had once been dauntless and dashing
Against all wild game, and had given his master
Constant service and satisfaction,
Began to grow feeble from the burden of the years.
One day, doing battle with a bristling boar,
He had got it by the ear, but it easily escaped
By twisting away from the decayed teeth.
The hunter, deprived of his expected prey,
Scolded his hound, who then countered:
"It's strength, not spirit, that's deserted me, master.
If you want to blame me for what I've become,
You should give me credit for what I was."

No need, I fancy, to stress the message.

PEROTTI'S APPENDIX *

---

* These additional fables were transcribed in the fifteenth century by the humanist Niccoló Perotti from a manuscript of Phaedrus now lost.

1. THE APE AND THE FOX
(Moral: that the miser does not willingly give away even what is
superfluous to his needs)

A monkey came moaning with dismay to the fox
And pleaded for part of that plentiful tail
To cover the embarrassment of his bare buttocks.
But the spiteful creature cruelly countered,
"If my tail were extended to twice its length,
I'd still rather trail it through briars and mire
Than part with the puniest portion of it to you."

2. THE AUTHOR
(About those who read this book)

These modest products of my playful Muse
Are acclaimed by all, the nice and the nasty.
The former's judgment is generous and genuine,
The latter's sly, from secret resentment.

3. THE AUTHOR

(Moral: that one should not aim at more than is proper)

If Mother Nature had made mankind
In accordance with my own concept of creation,
Our powers would be much more plentifully provided.
She'd have given us the gifts that generous Fortune
Has actually scattered among countless creatures:
The tremendous steady strength of the elephant,
The rush of the lion, the longevity of the raven,
The proud power of the battling bull,
And the tractable tameness of the swift horse.
And on top of all that, man would still have
His own intrinsic, distinctive intelligence.
Jove, very likely, is laughing on Olympus,
Having deliberately and designedly denied
These collected characteristics to humankind,
For fear that our effrontery would filch from himself
The scepter that exercises sway over the world.

So let us be grateful for the gifts given
By unconquered Jove, and continue contented
To live our allotted lives, and not
Set our minds on more than mortality permits.

4. MERCURY AND THE TWO WOMEN
(Another fable on the same subject)

Two women once unwittingly entertained
Mercury, in a mean and miserly manner.
One had a small son in the cradle,
The other practiced the profession of prostitute.
To give them a suitable compensation for their services,
Mercury, on the point of departure, pronounced:
"This guest before you is a god. I will give
To each of you instantly whatever you ask."
The mother begged for her boy to be brought
To manhood and maturity in a moment of time,
Fully bearded. The prostitute prayed
That all that she touched would come trailing after her.
Away went Mercury on his wings. The women
Dashed indoors: where, lo and behold,
The baby, now bearded, began to bawl.
While the whore was having a hearty laugh
At her friend's expense, her nostrils became blocked
By a mass of mucus. So, meaning to blow
Her nose, she gripped it with her fingers, and it followed
As she pulled and pulled it longer and longer,
Down and down until it grazed the ground;
And the friend she'd ridiculed had a rich revenge.

5–6. PROMETHEUS AND GUILE
(On truth and falsehood)

Prometheus once, the potter parent
Of a new generation, had fashioned the figure
Of Truth with meticulous attention to his art,
To make her the dispenser of law among men.
It so happened, he was suddenly summoned
To a meeting by the messenger of mighty Jupiter;
So he gave the guardianship of his workshop to Guile,
The treacherous apprentice he had just appointed.
This Guile, out of rivalry, when the time was ripe
Constructed a replica with cunning craftsmanship
Precisely the same in every particular.
With his masterpiece almost finished, he found
That he'd run out of clay to complete the feet.
At that point, Prometheus appeared on the scene,
And Guile, guilty and giving way to panic,
Rushed back and sat on the bench where he belonged.
Dumbfounded by the closeness of the copy, Prometheus
Was determined to keep the credit for his craftsmanship,
And so he inserted both statues in the kiln.
When both were baked, and the breath of life
Had been poured into the pair by Prometheus' power,
Sacred Truth stepped chastely forward,
While the unfinished effigy was fixed fast.
So the spurious image, the product of stealth,
Was called Falsehood, and when folk affirm
That she has no feet, I fully agree.

Counterfeits occasionally bring acclaim to men
At the start, for a time, but Truth itself
Comes to light infallibly in the long run.

7. THE AUTHOR
(What matters is the meaning behind the words)

Ixion in the story is rotated eternally
On a wheel: this whimsical warning tells us
That Fortune is unstable, and settled never.
Sisyphus expends all his energy
On pushing a stone up a steep mountain,
Only to find over and over
Again that on getting to the very verge
It falls back and frustrates his efforts,
Leaving him to lament his lost labor—
An emblem of the interminable misery of man.
Tantalus, standing thirsty in his stream,
Reminds us that the miserly, in the midst of their blessings,
Are unable to enjoy a single one.
The wicked daughters of Danaus are condemned
To carry water to a vast vat,
Which they fail to fill, it being full of holes:
All the more, what you lavish on luxury will be lost.
Tityos lies tied down over nine
Acres, with his liver everlastingly lost
To the ravening vulture, and everlastingly
Growing back to be gobbled again.
Moral: the more land a man possesses,
The more labor and misery it makes.
On purpose did the people of past ages
Conceal the truth under a cryptic cover,
That the wise should be aware, and the stupid go astray.

8. THE AUTHOR

(On Apollo's oracle)

Phoebus, god of Delphi and fair Parnassus,
Lay bare, I beg you, what is best for us humans.

Lo and behold, the hair of the holy
Priestess bristles, the tripods tremble,
Religious awe, with its queer and eerie
Rumble, rolls through the recesses of the cave,
The laurels flutter, and the light of day
Dims down. The divine spirit
Pronounces its message through the Pythian priestess:
"Nations of the world, mark well this message
Given for your good by the god of Delos:
Be pious, and pray to the deities of Olympus;
Defend to the death your dear country,
Your chaste wives, your children, and your parents;
Be armed to drive your enemies away;
Give your friends a helping hand and have
Mercy on men immersed in misery;
Go with the good and attack the treacherous;
Correct crime and condemn the impious;
Punish those prurient people who defile
Lawful marriage with lechery and license;
Shun the evil; trust none too much."

With which prescription, the pure priestess
Collapsed, desperate: desperate indeed,
For what she had said was a waste of words.

9. AESOP AND THE WRITER
(On a bad author praising himself)

A man had recited some rotten writings
To Aesop, containing some excessive compliments
To himself, at elaborate, infelicitous length.
So, eager to elicit the old man's opinion,
He asked anxiously, "Am I being arrogant?
I trust not. I'm confident in my talent."
Aesop, exhausted by interminably listening
To such sorry stuff, said in reply,
"I approve of your lavishing praise on yourself:
From no other quarter will it conceivably come."

10. POMPEY AND HIS SOLDIER
(How difficult it is to know a man)

Among the army of Pompeius Magnus
Was serving a soldier of stupendous size,
But whose sissified speech and mincing manner
Had marked him as a catamite unmistakably.
One night this character crouched in hiding,
Waiting to ambush the baggage animals
Of the army's commander, and succeeded in seizing
The mules that were carrying his collection of clothing,
Together with a huge hoard of gold
And silver. Rumors started to spread,
And soon the culprit was caught and accused,
And hustled away to the headquarters.
When Magnus demanded in an amazed tone,
"Did you, a comrade, have the colossal
Insolence to rob me?" the soldier spat
On his left hand, and spread the spittle
With his four fingers on the flattened palm:
"I'd hope that my eyes would ooze away
Just like this, General, if I touched your treasure."
So Pompey, a simple soul, decided
To acquit this disgrace to the camp: inconceivable,
So daring a deed from such a sissy.
Before long, a burly barbarian
Challenged our army to choose a champion
To come and confront him in single combat.
Panic reigned in the Roman ranks,
Each man, even the officers, afraid
That the fate of fighting might fall on him.

In the end, our friend, who in fact, though a fairy
In mien and posture, was a Mars in prowess,
Approached Pompey in front of his platform
And asked the general in his affected accent,
"What about me?" In this trying time
Pompey, impatient at the interruption,
Had him ejected. But just at this juncture
A senior officer on the staff suggested,
"Could we, perhaps, take a chance with this character?
He'd be no great loss, and you're less likely
To give rise to criticism that you rashly risked
A courageous contestant, which could be the case
If a brave one had the bad luck to be beaten."
So Magnus allowed him to accept the challenge.
He sallied forth, and in a split second
Before the eyes of the amazed army
He decapitated his fearsome foe
And returned in triumph. Congratulations
From Pompey: "It gives me great pleasure
To present you, soldier, with this crown for courage.
But I'd hope that my eyes would ooze away
(He continued, copying the crude gesture
With which the other had accompanied his oath)
If you're not the scoundrel who stole my stuff."

11. JUNO, VENUS, AND THE HEN
(Concerning the prurience of women)

When Juno was vaunting her chastity, and avowing
In the presence of gods and goddesses that the greatest
Glory to be gained by women in the world
Was to stay mated to the same man,
Venus, not controverting her but preferring
A playful refutation, to show that she
Was clearly one of a kind among women,
Questioned a hen in the following fashion:
"What quantity of food would it take to content you?"
"Anything you offered would be acceptable,
Provided, please, that you promised me permission
To scratch around for scraps with my claws."
"Would a peck of wheat be sufficient to stop you
From scratching?" "A peck, per se, would be plenty;
But, please, I must have permission to scratch."
"What would it take to stop you scratching
Altogether?" Then the creature confessed
That her real weakness had been revealed.
"It would be no good if you gave me a granary:
I'd scratch just the same." They say that Juno
Laughed generously at Venus' joke:
She was well aware that it was womankind
That the goddess's allegory was getting at.

12. THE BULLOCK AND THE OLD OX
(How vicious youth can be tamed)

The father of a family had a fierce-tempered son.
No sooner had he escaped from his parents' presence,
Than the boy began to beat the slaves
Terribly, with a temper totally ungoverned.
So Aesop fashioned a fable for the father:
"A yeoman was yoking with a young bullock
An old ox, who objected to being joined
With a partner so much more powerful, and pleaded
His old age and enervated strength.
'There's nothing to be afraid of,' said the farmer,
'My motive is not to make you labor—
On the contrary: I want you to control your companion,
Who's done endless harm with his heels and horns.'
The same in your situation. Be sure
To keep this boy constantly in your company,
And control his cruelty by your kind example.
Otherwise, I warn you, there's worse in store,
With your whole household up in arms."

13. AESOP AND THE VICTORIOUS BOXER
(How boasting may sometimes be checked)

The wise old Phrygian once witnessed
A boxer boasting how he'd beaten his opponent,
And asked if this adversary was actually the stronger.
"Rubbish," he replied, "the result proves it;
My strength was certainly superior to his."
"Then I can't see what credit you can claim," said Aesop,
"If you've won by worsting a weaker man.
We'd be better able to bear with your bragging
If you'd outdone a stronger by sheer skill."

PEROTTI'S
APPENDIX

14. THE ASS AND THE LYRE
(How genius is often lost through misfortune)

An ass saw a lyre lying in a field.
He tried the strings tentatively with his hoof:
They responded with sounds. "A sweet thing,"
He mused wistfully, "but wasted on one
Like me, who am ignorant of the musician's art.
If someone more skilful had stumbled on this,
Imagine the magical music he could make."

So genius must go often unnoticed
And be lost to fame by the fickleness of fortune.

15. THE WIDOW AND THE SOLDIER *

(The inconstancy and lustfulness of women)

There was once a widow woman, who lost
The husband she'd lived with long and lovingly,
And who kept his corpse carefully in a sarcophagus.
It appeared to be impossible to part her from him,
And she spent her existence sadly in the sepulchre,
Thus gaining the name of a nonpareil
Of wifely chastity. It chanced, meanwhile,
That some people who had pillaged Jupiter's temple
Paid on the cross for their crime of sacrilege.
To prevent their relations from removing their remains,
Soldiers were stationed as sentinels on the bodies,
Which were close to the sepulchre where the woman had
   confined herself.
One night, a watchman wanted some water
And asked for some from her serving girl:
This maid happened to be waiting on her mistress,
Who was going to bed. Giving way to her grief,
She'd prolonged her vigil late by lamplight.
The soldier espied through the slightly open
Door a lady, a dream of loveliness.
Immediately, the man became madly enamored,
Possessed by a passion impossible to control.
Compulsion and cunning found countless excuses
For meeting this marvel more and more often.
Drawn toward him by these daily encounters,
She gradually grew more gracious to the stranger,
Until, in the end, she admitted him to her intimacy
And became attached by the strongest of ties.

---

* This macabre story, which later became known all over Europe, is thought to have
originated in the east. Its two earliest occurrences in Latin are here and in Petronius,
Satyricon, 111–112. It is commonly known, from the location given to it in Petronius,
as *The Widow of Ephesus.*

PEROTTI'S
APPENDIX

While the soldier was spending more nights as a suitor
Than he was as a watchman, one of the bodies
During his duty disappeared from its cross.
Desperate, he described his dilemma to the lady,
And this paragon of wives said, "There's one way
To save you. Don't be afraid." And she gave him
Her husband's corpse to hoist on the cross,
So rescuing him from the penalty due for his default.
Thus was decency defeated by dishonor.

16. THE TWO SUITORS
(Fortune sometimes favors men beyond their wildest hopes)

Two young men were once wooing
The same girl. One of them was wealthy,
The other personable and patrician but poor.
The former was favored by the family of the girl.
When the day of the wedding duly dawned,
The lovelorn loser, laden with grief,
Made his way to his humble holding
Out in the country, close, by chance,
To the splendid mansion of the man getting married,
The wealthy one, which was waiting to receive
The maiden bride from her mother's bosom,
His city house being too small for the ceremony.
The wedding procession wended its way,
A crowd collected and the conjugal torch
Held by Hymen headed the company.
Now an ass, which provided the poor man with some profit,
Happened to be waiting at the gate of his hovel
When the wedding procession was passing that point.
The bride's brothers borrowed it, for hire,
To save their sister from spoiling her soft
Feet on the rough and dusty road.
Then suddenly the sky, by the saving grace
Of the goddess Venus, growled with thunder,
Was swept by winds, and went wild
With a tremendous tempest of torrential rain.
Dismal darkness reigned, and a hailstorm
Sent the wedding guests scattering for shelter.
The ass found its familiar refuge
Close at hand, and came clattering home
And proclaimed its presence with a piercing bray.

The servants emerged and were startled to see,
To their utter delight, a dazzling damsel.
They made this known immediately to their master,
Who was sitting inside, surrounded by friends,
Carousing with cup after cup of wine
To console himself for the sadness of his loss.
When the news was announced, he was a new man,
And with Bacchus and Venus buoying him up,
To the approbation and applause of his peers,
He ecstatically consummated his clandestine nuptials.
The bride's parents enquired everywhere
For their daughter's whereabouts, and the one designated
As her groom was given over to grief
For the loss of his lady. But later, when the public
Had heard the whole history, they hailed it
As a glorious favor granted by the gods.

17. AESOP AND HIS MISTRESS
(Moral: it is often harmful to speak the truth)

Aesop was working for a plain woman
Who wasted her days on making up her face,
Decked herself out in costly clothes
And garbed herself gaudily in gold and pearls—
And in spite of all that, not a single suitor
So much as touched her. So Aesop enquired,
"May I say something?" "Say on," she replied.
"I think you'd accomplish anything you aspired to,
  If you'd free yourself from those fripperies and fancies."
"Do you find my face so fetching unadorned?"
"On the contrary, if you gave up being generous with gifts,
  Your bed would feel better and benefit from the rest."
"Unlike your ribs," she riposted, and promptly
Ordered the free-tongued fellow to be flogged.
Soon afterward, a circlet of silver was stolen.
When the woman was informed that they'd failed to find it,
She summoned the staff, seething with rage,
And assured them they'd suffer the severest beating
If they didn't denounce the dastard responsible
And tell the truth. To which Aesop retorted,
"You can menace the others, mistress, as much
As you want. But it won't work against me.
I'm wise to your ways. I was viciously whipped
Some time ago because I told the truth."

18. THE COCK AND THE CATS WHO CARRIED HIS SEDAN CHAIR

(Too great a sense of security often leads men into danger)

A cock had some cats to carry his sedan.
When the fox saw him supported in such style,
He warned him: "You'd be wise to beware of treachery;
If you took a close look at those fellows' faces,
You'd come to the conclusion that they were carrying not
A load, as you think, but some luscious loot."
Too true. When the team of cats
Were feeling hungry in their feline fashion,
They dismembered their master and made themselves a meal.

19. THE SOW GIVING BIRTH AND THE WOLF
(You should always test a man before putting your trust in him)

When a sow was about to deliver her litter
And lay there groaning in the last moments,
A wolf came trotting up and offered his aid,
Declaring he was competent to carry out the duties
Of a midwife. But, aware of his wicked ways
And deceitful temperament, she rejected his tenders,
Suspecting services from that sinister source.
"It's quite enough," she countered, "if you keep
A safe distance away from my sty."

If she'd tamely trusted that treacherous wolf,
She'd still have experienced the pain of parturition,
Then lost her litter and her life as well.

20. AESOP AND THE RUNAWAY SLAVE
(One should not add trouble to trouble)

A slave escaping from a mean master
Encountered Aesop, whom he knew as a neighbor.
"Whatever's the trouble?" "I'll tell you truthfully,
Father (that's a term of address you deserve),
Since complaints can safely be consigned to your keeping:
Too much punishment, too little victuals.
Sometimes I'm sent to his faraway farm
With no rations to revive me on the road.
If he dines in, I stand in attendance
All night long. If he's invited out,
I doss down till dawn in the street.
The time for my liberty has long elapsed,
But hoary headed I'm still a slave.
If I felt I'd failed or was at fault at all,
I'd put up with it patiently. I'm permanently hungry,
And, to make my misery the more unbearable,
I'm bullied and battered by a brute of a master.
These are my main motives, among many,
For deciding to depart—to no definite place—
Anywhere away from this awful existence.
"Now, listen," said Aesop. "You've listed the tribulations
You say you suffer in spite of being guiltless.
But running away is wrong by the rules:
Think of the catastrophe you'll incur for that!"

This wise advice deflected him from his flight.

21. THE RACE HORSE
(One must bear with resignation whatever happens)

Someone once stole a splendid race horse,
Which had worked wonders and won prizes
For its team of four drawing the chariot,
And sold him, to make money, to a mill.
Being taken out from turning the stones
One day, for a drink, he descried his erstwhile
Team mates making their way to the race track
To give pleasure to spectators at the public games.
As the tears started to his eyes, he exclaimed,
"Good luck to you, lads! Go along without me,
Run a good race in the glamour of the games.
As for me, I'll return to the trials and torment
Of the sink where the scoundrel thievishly thrust me,
And lament the fate inflicted by Fortune."

22. THE HUNGRY BEAR
(Hunger sharpens the wits of creatures)

Whenever the bear, browsing in the woods,
Finds the supply of his food is failing,
He runs down shambling to the rocky shore
And lowers his legs little by little
Into the shoals of the water. And when the shaggy
Hair has been covered with clasping crabs,
He leaps back nimbly onto dry land,
Shakes loose the loot he's collected from the shallows
And cleverly feasts on the fabulous food.

Thus, hunger is a whetstone for the weakest wits.

23. THE TRAVELER AND THE RAVEN
(Men are often deceived by words)

A man was traveling down a lonely lane,
When he heard a voice hailing him, "Hullo!"
He paused a moment, and perceiving no one
He quickened his pace, and again the same
Sound greeted him from some unseen source.
The greeting was friendly, and feeling reassured
He stopped, to return the same civility
To whoever it was who was wishing him well.
When he'd looked in perplexity for a long time
In every direction, and spent enough
Time to have traveled a decent distance,
A crow accosted him, cruising overhead,
With another "Hullo!" When he saw the source,
And knew he'd been fooled, he furiously let fly,
"Horrible bird, to hell with your 'Hullos';
From lingering and listening to you, I'll be late."

24. THE SHEPHERD AND THE SHE-GOAT
(Nothing is so well hidden that it cannot be uncovered)

A shepherd, in gathering his goats together,
Struck a she-goat with his staff and shattered her horn.
He was begging her not to betray his brutality
To their master, when the creature cleverly countered:
"All right. You've damaged me, though I don't deserve it,
But I'll keep quiet when he comes to inspect us.
Still, the signs of your offense will speak for themselves."

25. THE SNAKE AND THE LIZARD

(When the lion's skin fails, you must put on the fox's; i.e., when you haven't the strength, you must use cunning)

A snake had succeeded in snatching a lizard
From behind, and was about to swallow it whole,
When the creature caught up a convenient twig,
And clamping it cross-wise in its clenched teeth
Established a barrier against being gobbled up
By this subtle scheme. The snake released it,
Unable to keep the creature he had caught.

26. THE CROW AND THE SHEEP
(Many molest the weak and give in to the strong)

An odious crow had settled on a sheep.
The sheep, after carrying it reluctantly on its back
For a long time, eventually protested:
"If you'd dared to do this, damn you, to a dog
   With strong teeth, he'd have taught you to regret it."
To which this worst of creatures countered,
"I despise the defenseless and defer to the strong.
   I know whom to harass and whom to flatter
   With wily words. That's why I'm able
   To prolong my life to limitless years."

27. SOCRATES AND THE RASCALLY SERVANT
(No curse is heavier than your own conscience)

A rascally slave was berating Socrates.
This man had a mistress—his master's wife—
And Socrates knew this was common knowledge
To the bystanders, and so got back at him: "Because
You please a person it's not proper to please,
You're satisfied with yourself. But don't be so smug.
The person whom you should properly please,
The censor inside you, you definitely don't."

28. THE HARE AND THE HERDSMAN
(Many people are amiable in words but treacherous at heart)

A hunter was harrying a hare, which escaped
But was spotted by a ploughman as it crept into a copse.
"Please, ploughman, don't point me out.
I've never done damage to this domain."
The ploughman replied, "I promise I won't;
Just stay under cover and keep quiet."
Up comes the hunter in hot pursuit,
"Hey, ploughman, has a hare been here?"
"Yes," he said, "but he went off to the left,"
But so saying, signed with his eyes to the right.
The hunter, in a hurry, missed the message
And disappeared into the distance. The deceitful ploughman
Asked, "Aren't you grateful that I gave you a getaway?"
"True enough, to your tongue I'm grateful.
But as to your eyes which attempted to ensnare me,
I'd love to see you stripped of their service."

29. THE COURTESAN AND THE YOUNG MAN
(Many things please us which are, nevertheless, troublesome)

When a sly courtesan was trying to seduce
A young fellow who'd found her faithless
And been much misled many a time,
He still submitted slavishly to her charms.
Whereupon the wily woman wheedled him,
"No matter how many compete in courting me,
And try to attract me with their tempting bribes,
You're still the man who means most to me."
The youth, reflecting how often he'd been fooled,
Declared, "I'm delighted, darling, to hear it.
Not that I trust your truthfulness at all,
But because, all the same, you bring me such bliss."

30. THE BEAVER

(Many people would live on, if they would abandon their fortunes in order to save their lives)

When a beaver's unable to baffle the hounds
And escape from their clutches (the garrulous Greeks,
Who vaunt themselves on their versatile vocabulary,
Call him *castor*, conferring on the creature
The name of a god), the saying goes
That he bites off his ballocks, being aware
They're the prize his pursuers are at pains to procure.
About this belief of the beaver's there's something
Divinely prompted, I don't deny it.
For as soon as he's seized the specific he was after,
The huntsman is happy, and the hounds are called off.
If men could somehow sacrifice their possessions,
They'd be likely to live long and safely.
No one would plot against a person without property.

31. THE BUTTERFLY AND THE WASP
(We should direct our attention to our present fortune, not our past one)

A butterfly saw a wasp buzzing about
Nearby, and reflected, "How unlucky is my lot!
While the bodies from whose relics we both were born
Still were living, I was eloquent in peace,
Brave in battle, and outstanding in the arts:
Now I'm winging my way weightless and worthless.
You, in the past a pack mule, are privileged
To select any victim and sting him viciously." *
But the wasp spoke words worth remembering:
"Remove the past from your mind. What matters
Is what we are now, not what we were."

---

* This fable is based on the doctrine of the transmigration of souls. The butterfly in his last existence was, by inference, a distinguished human being. The wasp was a pack mule. Possibly, Phaedrus sees himself as the stinging wasp, the moralist and satirist.

PEROTTI'S
APPENDIX

32. THE GROUND SWALLOW AND THE FOX
(One should not trust scoundrels)

There's a bird that's called by our country cousins
The ground swallow—because it builds
The nest for its eggs on the level earth.
Well, one of them was waylaid by a wicked fox,
And as soon as she saw it, she soared into the air.
"Flying away?" said the fox, "You're afraid of me?
I've masses to maintain me in this meadow without you.
There are plenty of beetles and lots of locusts,
And crickets galore. You've no cause to escape.
I'm particularly impressed by your peaceful behavior
And settled existence." The songbird countered,
"Fine words. But I'm wise enough to know
That I can't compete with you down on the ground,
While up in the air I'm easily your equal.
Fly up and follow me. I'll be friendly up here."